The Encyclopedia of
Collectibles

TIME
LIFE ®
BOOKS

Other Publications:

The Seafarers

World War II

The Great Cities

Home Repair and Improvement

The World's Wild Places

The Time-Life Library of Boating

Human Behavior

The Art of Sewing

The Old West

The Emergence of Man

The American Wilderness

The Time-Life Encyclopedia of Gardening

Life Library of Photography

This Fabulous Century

Foods of the World

Time-Life Library of America

Time-Life Library of Art

Great Ages of Man

Life Science Library

The Life History of the United States

Time Reading Program

Life Nature Library

Life World Library

Family Library:
    How Things Work in Your Home
    The Time-Life Book of the Family Car
    The Time-Life Family Legal Guide
    The Time-Life Book of Family Finance

The Encyclopedia of
Collectibles
Children's Books to Comics

TIME-LIFE BOOKS, ALEXANDRIA, VIRGINIA

Time-Life Books Inc.
is a wholly owned subsidiary of
TIME INCORPORATED

Founder: Henry R. Luce 1898-1967

Editor-in-Chief: Hedley Donovan
Chairman of the Board: Andrew Heiskell
President: James R. Shepley
Vice Chairman: Roy E. Larsen
Corporate Editors: Ralph Graves,
Henry Anatole Grunwald

TIME-LIFE BOOKS INC.
Managing Editor: Jerry Korn
Executive Editor: David Maness
Assistant Managing Editors: Dale M. Brown,
Martin Mann, John Paul Porter
Art Director: Tom Suzuki
Chief of Research: David L. Harrison
Director of Photography: Robert G. Mason
Planning Director: Thomas Flaherty (acting)
Senior Text Editor: Diana Hirsh
Assistant Art Director: Arnold C. Holeywell
Assistant Chief of Research: Carolyn L. Sackett

Chairman: Joan D. Manley
President: John D. McSweeney
Executive Vice Presidents: Carl G. Jaeger (U.S.
and Canada), David J. Walsh (International)
Vice President and Secretary: Paul R. Stewart
Treasurer and General Manager:
John Steven Maxwell
Business Manager: Peter G. Barnes
Sales Director: John L. Canova
Public Relations Director: Nicholas Benton
Personnel Director: Beatrice T. Dobie
Production Director: Herbert Sorkin
Consumer Affairs Director: Carol Flaumenhaft

The Encyclopedia of Collectibles
Editor: Betsy Frankel
Chief Researcher: Phyllis K. Wise
Researchers: Michael Blumenthal, Trudy Pearson,
Judith W. Shanks
Editorial Assistant: Susan Sivard

Editorial Production
Production Editor: Douglas B. Graham
Operations Manager: Gennaro C. Esposito
Assistant Production Editor: Feliciano Madrid
Quality Control: Robert L. Young (director),
James J. Cox (assistant),
Michael G. Wight (associate)
Art Coordinator: Anne B. Landry
Copy Staff: Susan B. Galloway (chief),
Peter Kaufman, Cynthia Kleinfeld,
Ricki Tarlow, Florence Keith, Celia Beattie
Picture Department: Dolores A. Littles
Correspondents: Elisabeth Kraemer (Bonn); Margot
Hapgood, Dorothy Bacon (London); Susan Jonas,
Lucy T. Voulgaris (New York); Maria Vincenza
Aloisi, Josephine du Brusle (Paris); Ann Natanson
(Rome). Valuable assistance was also provided by
Carolyn T. Chubet, Miriam Hsia (New York).

The Encyclopedia of Collectibles
was created under the supervision
of Time-Life Books by
TREE COMMUNICATIONS, INC.
President: Rodney Friedman
Publisher: Bruce Michel
Vice President: Ronald Gross
Secretary: Paul Levin

The Encyclopedia of Collectibles
Editor: Andrea DiNoto
Text Director: Jay Gold
Art Director: Sara Burris
Assistant Text Editor: Linda Campbell Franklin
Photographers: David Arky, Steven Mays
Assistant Editor: Cathy Cashion
Assistant Art Director: Christopher Jones
Chief Researcher: Catherine Ireys
Researchers: Anna-Teresa Callen, Mary Clarke,
Alix Gudefin, Laura James, Enid Klass,
Judson Mead, Barbara Moynehan,
Dennis Southers, Henry Wiencek
Administrative Assistants: Eva Gold, Silvia Kelley
Writers: Ann Cameron, Francis Carpenter,
Carol Wald, Hyla Clark, Sally Clark

Consultants for this volume: Linda Lapidus
(Children's Books); Mary Lewis (Chinese Export
Porcelain); Maggie Rogers (Christmas Tree
Ornaments); Fred Bradley (Cigar Labels and
Bands); Bob Parkinson (Circus Memorabilia); Lee
Wallace (Civil War Equipment); Chris Bailey,
Henry Fried (Clocks); Elvira and Vladimir Clain-
Stefanelli (Coins); Margaret Kimball Herlihy
(Combs); Bill Blackbeard, Jim Ivey, Chuck Wooley
(Comics)

The Cover: Comic-book characters from comic
strips, the classics and science fiction suggest the
broad range of this category of collectibles.

Acknowledgments: Hexagonal plate, page 24,
caddy, page 25, all material, pages 26-27, shell
dish, page 30, and detail, page 32, courtesy
Museum of the American China Trade; Omar
label, page 48, and label, page 59, courtesy Ellery
Karl; Virginia label, page 51, courtesy Mr. and
Mrs. J. W. Gilbert; Wilson and Washington bands,
page 55, courtesy Carol Wald; buttons, page 82,
courtesy Alphaeus Albert; stereoview, page 85,
courtesy Alan and Hilary Weiner; label, page 89,
English clock (detail), page 90, steeple clock, page
92, Jerome clock, page 98, Gila clock, page 99,
courtesy American Clock and Watch Museum,
Inc., Bristol, Connecticut; painted clocks, page 98,
courtesy Clock Hutt, Ltd.; coins, pages 116-139,
courtesy American Numismatic Society; wampum,
page 128, courtesy Museum of the American
Indian, Heye Foundation; Gasoline Alley, page
149, Little Orphan Annie and the Teenie Weenies,
pages 150-151, courtesy Chicago Tribune-New
York News Syndicate; Blondie comic strip, page
151, ©King Features Syndicate; toys, pages 152-
153, courtesy Robert Lesser; Felix the Cat, page
153, ©Felix the Cat Productions Inc.; Dagwood
and Popeye toys, page 153, ©King Features
Syndicate; Superman toy used by arrangement
with DC Comics Inc.; Sensation Comics No. 1,
©1941, renewed 1968, DC Comics Inc., Special
Edition Comics No. 1 used by arrangement with
DC Comics Inc., Detective Comics No. 33, ©1939,
renewed 1966, DC Comics Inc., Superman No. 1,
©1939, renewed 1966, DC Comics Inc., all page
155; comics, pages 155-160, courtesy Robert
Lesser and William Emerson.

Contents

LITTLE BOYS AND GIRLS

A B C

Children's Books
Beloved Relics of Early Reading

Although the collecting of adult books is an avocation centuries old, it was only during the 1940s that numbers of people discovered the charm of acquiring old books written or illustrated for the young. This interest in children's books grew quickly, and the prices of good editions of celebrated works skyrocketed. In 1965 I bought first editions of all four volumes in the famous *Winnie-the-Pooh* series by the British author A. A. Milne for $10 to $15 each. Barely a decade later the set of four books was bringing $400.

Despite this rush of interest, the field is anything but combed over. Millions of interesting and valuable vol-

---

John Hayes, a theater producer in Canada, began collecting children's books in 1958. His collection includes volumes from many periods, but is richest in volumes from Victorian times and the early 20th Century.

---

umes must be undiscovered in storerooms and secondhand bookstores. On a visit to London I went into a bookshop to inquire if they stocked secondhand children's books. The proprietor said no, but added as an afterthought, "There are some we just acquired, but have not yet sorted and priced. You are welcome to look in the basement." I felt like the astonished discoverer of King Tut's tomb. There before me were at least 250 children's books, mostly pre-1910 fairy tales, all looking as new as they did the day they came off the press. Once owned by a book-loving bachelor, they had never been handled by grubby young hands.

The ones you are most likely to find in bookshops and attics are children's books published since the middle of the 19th Century. Before 1850 young people's books—called juveniles by publishers—tended to be more like schoolbooks and religious tracts than imaginative children's literature. The first children's books, which were published in England in the 17th and early 18th centuries, were primarily ABC books, collections of sermons and the like. However, because of their age, and the tendency of children to mistreat their books, not very many of them have survived. If you are fortunate enough

A century after publication, an American alphabet book retains its bright colors. It was produced by McLoughlin Brothers of New York, a firm that pioneered lavish color printing in children's books.

to come across one, you will have a valuable prize.

In the mid-18th Century a London publisher named John Newbery sugar-coated the heavy messages in diverting prose and verse. But children's literature did not flower until about 1850, when Edward Lear wrote his marvelous nonsense rhymes, and an obscure mathematics professor named Charles Lutwidge Dodgson dubbed himself Lewis Carroll and produced *Alice's Adventures in Wonderland* and its sequel, *Through the Looking Glass.* These imaginative volumes were among the earliest to help establish the tradition of fine children's literature.

Almost any book from those early days will be an interesting addition to your library, but many collectors specialize—in antique miniatures from centuries past, in books about animals, in the various editions of works by a favorite author such as Lewis Carroll, in volumes with desirable illustrations. A few favor what are called Robinsonades—books like *The Swiss Family Robinson* that have been inspired by, and play variations on, *Robinson Crusoe.* Serious collectors look for several especially desirable types of juvenile literature. The first is simply "classics"—the books almost everyone remembers.

One of the rarest and most desirable of the classics is L. Frank Baum's *The Wonderful Wizard of Oz.* It is not very old. The first edition of this first of the 13 Oz books written by Baum (after his death other authors added another 30 or so titles) was published by Geo. M. Hill Co. in 1900, and copies must still be hidden in many American attics. It can be recognized by an error, later corrected, on page 14: the first line reads "low wail on" instead of "low wail of." One copy that was found was advertised for sale in a 1970 catalogue for $1,250. Another valuable classic is *Little Women.* The first edition of Louisa May Alcott's memorable book about a family of girls, offered by Roberts Brothers in 1868 for $1.25, was worth $1,000 a century later. Only 2,000 copies were printed, but it was such a success that Miss Alcott extended the story and later editions were printed as two volumes, so marked on the spines.

There are dozens of such immortal children's tales. The most beloved by Americans are probably Mark Twain's *The Adventures of Tom Sawyer* and its companion volume, *The Adventures of Huckleberry Finn* (the latter is a profound adult novel but has also become a favorite with the young). *Tom Sawyer* was first published in 1876 in Britain by Chatto & Windus and in the United States by the American Publishing Company, and the authentic first printing has the title on a separate page; the title was later moved to the reverse of the frontispiece. The first edition of *Huckleberry Finn*, dated 1885, is recognizable in line 23 of page 57: the word "saw" is misprinted as "was." Less than a century later *Huckleberry Finn* was worth more than $500 and *Tom Sawyer* over $2,000.

There is considerable variation in rarity—and therefore value—of even these 19th Century classics. A first edition of Robert Louis Stevenson's *Kidnapped* (1886), for example, increased in value over a century or so to $250, but Stevenson's *Treasure Island* (1883) brought about three times as much. Hundred-year-old books are not easy to locate, but many books that are recent enough to have been bought for your own children have become sought-after prizes. Some examples are Milne's stories of Winnie-the-Pooh, James Thurber's *The White Deer,* and E. B. White's *Charlotte's Web* and *Stuart Little. Charlotte's Web,* a book that sold new for $2.50 in 1952, was worth $50 by 1977 if it was a first edition (you can tell by looking on the copyright page, which in the first printing has the letters "I-B").

Large quantities of these recent books were printed and many must survive. But far more numerous originally were mass-produced adventure stories disdained in literary circles. The Horatio Alger rags-to-riches stories of the 1870s are now much sought after, but later series are generally overlooked as inconsequential. Probably the most interesting are the Tom Swift and Hardy Boys adventure stories for boys and the Nancy Drew mysteries for girls. All these titles were turned out by a story factory with a half dozen writers scribbling at once under the direction, first, of Edward Stratemeyer and later of his daughter, Harriet Stratemeyer Adams. The rarest volumes are the first five Tom Swifts—*Tom Swift and His Motor Cycle, His Motor Boat, His Air Ship, His Submarine Boat* and *His Electric Runabout*—all brought out simultaneously in 1910. The first three of the Nancy Drews—*The Secret of the Old Clock, The Hidden Staircase* and *The Bungalow Mystery,* all published in 1930—are desirable, as are the initial Hardy Boys books of 1927, *The Tower Treasure, The House on the Cliff* and *The Secret of the Old Mill.* First editions of these much-loved tales still may be picked up relatively cheaply.

Akin to these stories are the many Tarzan books produced by the prolific Edgar Rice Burroughs. His first Tarzan tale, *Tarzan of the Apes,* eventually sold 25 million copies, but the first edition of 1914, published by A. C. McClurg & Co. of Chicago, is rare and was worth in excess of $250 a half century later. First editions of sequels, such as *The Beasts of Tarzan* (1915), also have value. The early Disney books are also rare. One of the first, a slender volume called *The Adventures of Mickey Mouse, Book I* (McKay, 1931) that originally cost 50 cents sold in 1976 for $55.

Many old and not-so-old children's books are valuable less for their literary merits, if any, than for their artistic qualities. Picture books and heavily illustrated volumes of all kinds have understandably been staples of publishers. A number of the artists were very talented, considerable expense was invested in production and the results in many cases are charming prizes for the collector. Even in the 19th and early 20th centuries, when color printing was much more difficult and less common than it is today, many children's books were published with fine color pictures. Most were done by lithography, the process then used to produce color labels and advertisements, but a number involved other techniques. A few *(page 11)* were printed in black and white and colored by hand. For others woodcuts—one made by hand for each primary color in each picture—were employed, and for a few of the last issues of the famous Kate Greenaway *Almanack (page 8),* the newly introduced and costly process of color photogravure was used.

Among the more desirable of the illustrated books, of course, are the ones that combine literary and artistic merit. Deluxe editions of standard favorites—*Tom Sawyer, Treasure Island, The Last of the Mohicans, Robinson Crusoe*—were published earlier in this century with illustrations by such artists as Howard Pyle, Norman Rockwell and, best of all, N. C. Wyeth (father of the contemporary painter Andrew Wyeth), whose Indians were nobler and pirates more villainous than anybody else's. Many notable classics illustrated by Wyeth were published in a series by Charles Scribner's Sons, which marked its first printings with the letter "A" on the title page. Other classic illustrations include original drawings made for Lewis Carroll's Alice books by Sir John Tenniel, and E. H. Shepard's illustrations for the Pooh books and for Kenneth Grahame's *The Wind in the Willows.* Arthur Rackham, another top illustrator, did many books, including Washington Irving's tales.

As with other sorts of book collecting, first editions in good condition command higher prices than later editions or battered copies. But these factors are not as crucial to the collectors of children's books as they are to people who look for adult volumes. Nobody expects books that have been handled by children to be pristine and unmarked. Modern books are more valuable if untouched and in their original dust jackets, but older volumes can be a bit dog-eared and still be acceptable; it is in the nature of children's books to have been loved half to death by their enthusiastic readers.

For related material, see the article on Books in a separate volume of this encyclopedia.

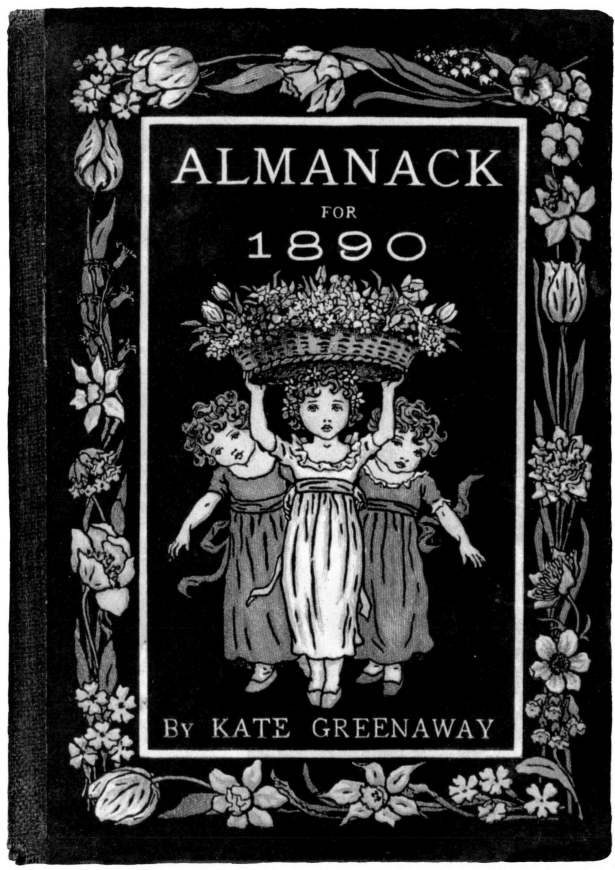

Reproduced above at more than twice its actual size—3 by 4 inches—is the 1890 edition of the popular "Almanacks" by Kate Greenaway, whose demure little girls made her one of the more popular illustrators of the late 1800s. The "Almanacks," with calendars and verses, were published in London annually from 1883 to 1895 by George Routledge, but the rarest is one issued, after a year's hiatus, by J. M. Dent in 1897.

The name of the author adds to the value of the *1860 book containing the illustration at right, in which Reynard, the rascally fox of folklore, poses as a pious pilgrim bound for Rome and receives the blessing of a ram cleric while a hare holds a Bible. Such animal tales, told and retold since medieval times, were written down for children in the 18th Century by many hacks. But the version with this picture is by the great German poet-philosopher Johann Wolfgang von Goethe.*

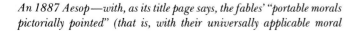

An 1887 Aesop—with, as its title page says, the fables' "portable morals pictorially pointed" (that is, with their universally applicable moral lessons illustrated)—is especially notable for the pictorial painting, in color, by British artist Walter Crane.

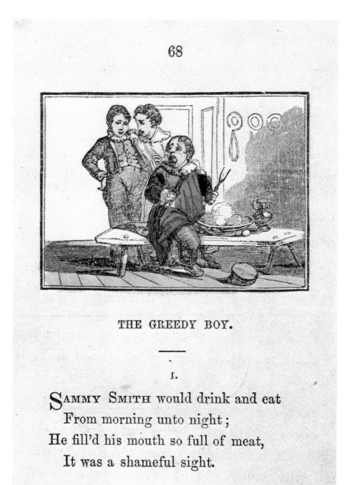

68

THE GREEDY BOY.

—

I.

SAMMY SMITH would drink and eat
From morning unto night;
He fill'd his mouth so full of meat,
It was a shameful sight.

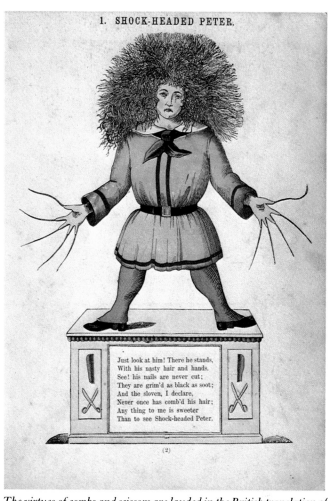

1. SHOCK-HEADED PETER.

Just look at him! There he stands,
With his nasty hair and hands.
See! his nails are never cut;
They are grim'd as black as soot;
And the sloven, I declare,
Never once has comb'd his hair;
Any thing to me is sweeter
Than to see Shock-headed Peter.

(2)

Comic illustration and rhymed verse soften the moral message in this 1835 English book aimed at teaching the young good manners.

The virtues of combs and scissors are lauded in the British translation of "Struwelpeter," a famous German good-grooming book.

Girls are advised to act suitably feminine and obedient in an 1860 deportment book called "The Little Minxes." The pages at left and right

show the consequences of playing the tomboy, while at center a girl wastes away because she gave her medicine to the cat instead of taking it herself.

7

A demure mouse plays the piano for a red-coated frog (top) in a comic, colorful illustration for the song "Froggie Would a-Wooing Go" that appears in the 1875 "A Book of Drolleries." By this time many children's books aimed more to amuse than to teach or preach.

Below and at right are illustrations by Randolph Caldecott for two Mother Goose stories. Caldecott, who died in 1886, is one of the most admired of children's artists; an annual prize for illustration is given in his name.

There was an old man, who when little
Fell casually into a kettle;
But, growing too stout, He could never get out,
So he passed all his life in that kettle.

Jack Sprat and his Wife. 115

Jack Sprat could eat no fat,
 His wife could eat no lean;
And so betwixt them both, you see,
 They licked the platter clean.

 Pretty John Watts,
 We are troubled with rats—
Will you drive them out of the house?
 We have mice, too, in plenty,
 That feast in the pantry;
But let them stay and nibble away—
What harm in a little brown mouse?

A drawing by Edward Lear illustrates one of his own imaginative limericks in an 1872 book he titled "More Nonsense Pictures, Rhymes, etc."

Jack Sprat and his wife appear with their clean platter in an 1890 Mother Goose that also includes a rhyme defending mice.

Tales retold by the folklorist Andrew Lang—"The Olive Fairy Book" (left, rear), "The Brown Fairy Book" (foreground) and "The Blue Fairy Book"—are valued for his artistry and for the beautiful bindings and printing. Below are the frontispiece and title page of Lang's best-known original work, "The Princess Nobody," published in 1884.

THE

PRINCESS NOBODY

A

TALE OF FAIRY LAND

BY

ANDREW LANG

AFTER THE DRAWINGS BY RICHARD DOYLE

PRINTED IN COLOURS BY EDMUND EVANS

LONDON
LONGMANS, GREEN AND CO.

BELLEROPHON ON PEGASVS

An 1892 edition of Nathaniel Hawthorne's "A Wonder Book for Boys and Girls" is prized for the illustrations by Walter Crane. The frontispiece (above) shows Pegasus, the winged horse of Greek myth, carrying the hero Bellerophon.

An 1890 version of Lewis Carroll's "Alice's Adventures in Wonderland," called "The Nursery Alice," includes 20 of John Tenniel's original pictures, like the Queen of Hearts (above, right), but has a less inspired cover by E. Gertrude Thomson.

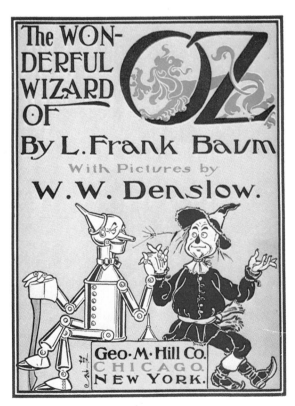

A bright picture of Cock Robin's wedding procession illustrates an 1888 American edition of the sad English medieval tale.

The title page of the rare 1900 first edition of "The Wonderful Wizard of Oz" pictures the Scarecrow and the Tin Man.

NOT A WINK THE WHOLE NIGHT LONG

The princess proves herself royal by detecting the pea hidden under stacked mattresses in a version of "The Princess and the Pea," published in a World War I-era anthology of children's stories noteworthy for its fine illustrations by Edmund Dulac.

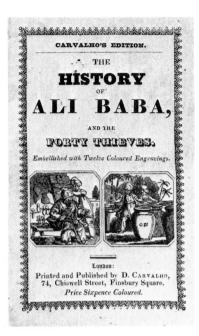

Horatio Alger's Tattered Tom—his only serial starring a girl—is so rare that a first edition seldom comes on the market.

"Sinbad the Sailor" is a "chapbook," which was cheaply printed to be sold on the street by peddlers called chapmen.

Although Carvalho's "The History of Ali Baba" cost only sixpence in 1830, it contained 12 engravings, each colored by hand.

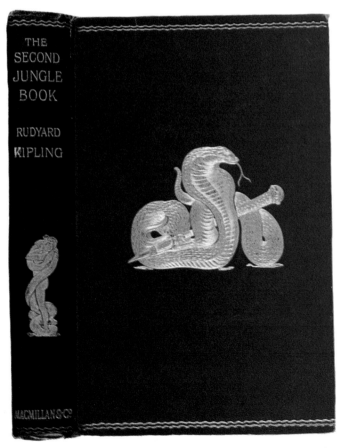

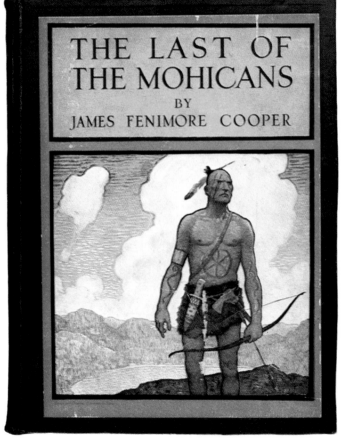

A handsome binding sets off this edition of Rudyard Kipling's "The Second Jungle Book," published in New York in 1895.

N. C. Wyeth pictures, including the cover, are the big attraction of this 1925 edition of a Cooper novel, one of many classics Wyeth illustrated.

EoR   Tigger   Kanga   Rabbit   WOL   Piglet   POOH   Christopher Robin

Playful end papers by E. H. Shepard complete the 1928 first edition of A. A. Milne's modern classic, "The House at Pooh Corner." This was the last Pooh book; the first, "When We Were Very Young" (1924), is rarest.

LIBRARIES

The Free Library of Philadelphia
Philadelphia, Pennsylvania 19103

University of Minnesota
The Kerlan Collection
Minneapolis, Minnesota 55455

Toronto Public Library
The Osborne Collection of Early Children's Books
Toronto, 5, Canada

The Philip H. and A. S. W. Rosenbach Foundation
Philadelphia, Pennsylvania 19103

The Pierpont Morgan Library
New York, New York 10016

PERIODICALS

AB Bookman's Weekly, AB Bookman Publications, Inc., Clifton, New Jersey 07015

The Horn Book Magazine, The Horn Book Inc., Boston, Massachusetts 02116

Phaedrus: A Journal of Children's Literature Research, Phaedrus, Inc., Boston, Massachusetts 02208

BOOKS

Bader, Barbara, *American Picturebooks from Noah's Ark to the Beast Within.* Macmillan, Inc., 1976.

Blanck, Jacob N., *Peter Parley to Penrod.* Mark Press Incorporated, 1974.

Darton, F. H., *Children's Books in England.* Cambridge University Press, 1932.

Meigs, Cornelia, ed., *A Critical History of Children's Literature.* Macmillan, Inc., 1969.

Muir, Percy, *English Children's Books 1600 to 1900.* B. T. Batsford Ltd., 1954.

Quayle, Eric, *The Collector's Book of Children's Books.* Clarkson N. Potter, Inc., 1971.

Targ, William, ed., *Bibliophile in the Nursery: A Bookman's Treasury of Collector's Lore on Old and Rare Children's Books.* Scarecrow Press, Inc., 1960.

Thwaite, Mary, *From Primer to Pleasure.* The Horn Book, Inc., 1972.

This tea bowl and saucer set was made for the American market. Its restrained, monochromatic color scheme, abundance of undecorated white space, and naïvely rendered, sparrow-like American eagles help to identify the pieces as examples of export porcelain made about 1790.

The coat of arms of George Washington's English kin decorates this armorial plate from around 1760. The stylized ornamentation at the rim, red and blue enamels and lavish use of gold mark this as a fine example of the Chinese ware called rose-colored.

Chinese Export Porcelain
Oriental Ware for Western Taste

As long ago as the Ninth Century A.D., word of the wonders of Chinese porcelain began to filter westward. Suleiman, a Muslim traveler in the East, wrote: "They have in China a very fine clay with which they make vases as transparent as glass; even water can be seen through them." Five centu-

John Quentin Feller, Professor of History at the University of Scranton, began collecting Chinese Export Porcelain in 1962. He has an entire dinner set of Rose Medallion plus a 300-piece collection.

ries later, Marco Polo spoke with equal amazement of the remarkably thin, translucent, pure-white ceramics he had seen in Cathay—like nothing ever created in Europe, he assured his readers. In time Europe did, of course, learn the secret of making fine porcelain. But many collectors still prefer such Chinese patterns as Canton and Rose Medallion, my own areas of specializa-

tion, for beauty, variety and craftsmanship. Add to that a rousing history of East-West trade relations, of which these pieces form the chief visual record, and you have a category of collectibles seldom equaled for fascination.

With few exceptions, the porcelain patterns collected today and in the past were made specifically for export from the 17th to the late 19th centuries, when upheavals in China and competition from Europe halted the business. Except for the earliest pieces, the export porcelains were generally distinguishable from ceramics made for the Chinese market, having been adapted in style, shape, color and subject to suit Western tastes. Often

A late example of rose palette in the Rose Medallion style, the plate at right was made about 1860. Like most Rose Medallion pieces, it combines motifs of birds, chrysanthemums and butterflies with alternating scenes of Chinese domestic life.

20

they were also of somewhat heavier porcelain, so they would withstand the rough ocean voyage between China and their destinations in Europe and America.

Most export porcelain was manufactured in the city of Ching-te Chen in the province of Kiangsi, about 600 miles distant from the port of Canton. The early pieces were also ornamented in Ching-te Chen, but as the manufacturing techniques changed and as Western merchants required more and more custom work, the painting phase of the operation was moved to Canton.

When the Portuguese opened the trade in porcelain and other exotic goods around 1520, Ching-te Chen was dominated by a royal pottery for the Ming emperors; only a few private potteries operated there. By the end of the 18th Century, after the Dutch and the British and, belatedly, the Americans had taken over the majority of the export business, "Porcelain City" had grown to include 3,000 independent manufacturers. Many of the city's estimated one million people were engaged in gathering and refining the raw materials that nature provided in the area—an unusually pure, white clay called kaolin that made the "flesh" or body of the porcelain; a superior grade of the mineral feldspar, called petuntse, that contributed the translucence and provided

A bridge, a teahouse and weeping willow mark this handsome plate as classic Canton, a style widely imported in late-18th Century America. A fine openwork border makes this piece especially valuable.

A 1795 coffeepot in the "lighthouse" shape made for European tastes is ornamented in a style called Nanking—like Canton but with refinements: a post-and-spear border, twisted strap handles and gilt overlay.

This openwork fruit bowl and underdish is fancier than most Canton ware, although it bears the characteristic border decoration—a scalloped line tracing the inside of the blue rim.

the glaze; and cobalt and copper oxide to make the blue and red pigments that were applied before firing and were the basic underglaze colors of early export ware.

Thousands of other citizens labored in the factories, which divided the production of each piece among as many as 50 or 60 workers. Each did no more than shape the foot of a vessel, for example, or paint a single repeating element of a design. The final step in the manufacture of early wares was application of the glaze coating, and its firing for three or four days in kilns heated to 2,300°F. or higher. The porcelain emerged with the glaze thoroughly fused to the body to form a hard, vitreous, supremely smooth and lustrous whole. Experimentation in the 17th and 18th centuries produced a rainbow of additional colors—including the subtle and much-desired rose palette, also called *famille rose*.

At first the Europeans had been content to take their porcelains pretty much in the shapes, sizes and styles the Chinese made for themselves. But as time passed they began to demand items better suited to their own tables and customs—tankards, coffeepots, soup tureens and eggcups—for which they supplied wooden models or actual samples. They also began to place custom orders for armorial plates carrying coats of arms, an organization's

A lozenge-shaped serving dish is made of celadon, a hard ceramic only slightly less fine than true porcelain. The celadon's characteristic gray-green glaze was decorated with Rose Medallion flora and fauna motifs.

Despite differences in color, each of the three pieces above has characteristics of the Fitzhugh pattern, named after a family of British sailor-merchants who bought quantities of china in this design. All are decorat-

ed with pictures of chrysanthemums and borders that include trelliswork. The square plate and pot de crème are fairly common, but the variation in the tureen border makes it unusual.

insignia or simply, as in the instance of many American orders, a family's monogram. Usually some decorative element from the Chinese repertoire was also incorporated into the overall design, with results that make a curious, if usually harmonious, mélange of styles.

Armorial pieces *(below, opposite, and page 30)* are prized items among collectors of Chinese export porcelain; the American eagle and other patriotic motifs *(page 20)* are others. Armorial pieces are the easiest Chinese export porcelain to date accurately—through family records, which may indicate when the ware was ordered or paid for. Sometimes the borders and other ornamentation appearing on the pieces can be used as clues to dating stock pieces. For example, it is known from easily dated, special-order pieces that the Blue Trellis border *(page 31)* was used by Chinese porcelain decorators only in the last decades of the 19th Century. Potters' marks and various other inscriptions that occasionally appear on the backs of pieces provide few and unreliable clues.

Much easier to find at affordable prices are several patterns produced during the late 1700s and the 1800s. Among the most common are two similar stock patterns, Canton and Nanking, which were exported in great quantity to America and were so inexpensive as to find their way to families of even modest means. Some ship captains dismissed them as "ballast ware," since they were stowed deep in the damp hold as flooring for more fragile and expensive teas and silks. Both Canton and the fancier Nanking styles depict a stylized Chinese landscape, with trees, a shrine, a pagoda, a bridge and, in some Nanking ware, a figure or two, all in a single underglaze blue on white. Another 19th Century pattern popular in the United States, and thus fairly easy to find, is Fitzhugh, named for a British family long in the China trade; it comes in several monochromes *(page 23)*.

As available and as popular as Canton and Nanking are two other export porcelains, both 19th Century evolutions of rose palette: Rose Medallion and Mandarin. Rose Medallion is distinguished by its center ornament or medallion, and by an overall floral and gold field interrupted by distinct open spaces, or reserves, so called because they were reserved for ornamentation with birds, fruits, flowers, butterflies and Chinese figures. Mandarin recapitulates similar elements, often with a distinct border and a central design of several Chinese figures in a classical imperial court setting.

Collectors will find the best opportunities for buying Chinese export porcelain around cities that were 19th Century ports on the East Coast, where most of these pieces first appeared. More than a million pieces of porcelain arrived in the West each year at the height of the trade, so it is not being unduly optimistic to assume that many more first-rate examples will come down from attics and closets and onto the market in years to come.

This octagonal gray-and-gilt plate from the Museum of the American China Trade bears an armorial escutcheon identifying the English families of Vaughan and Hallowell, and was made about 1750.

A Rose Medallion plate of 1830 with the MacPherson crest at center carries the legend, "Touch not the Cat but a Clove," the artist's shaky transcription of the family motto: "Touch not the cat but with a glove."

The Mandarin plate at left is part of a service owned by Betsy Patterson of Baltimore, who married Jerome Bonaparte—Napoleon's brother—in 1803. It carries the Bonaparte device of a pelican (top) and the motto "Fidelitas." The other plate bears the monogram of Jerome's grandson.

The arms of John Hanbury, a Quaker merchant of London who owned land in Virginia, decorate this jug, made around 1735.

This tea caddy displays a tiny anthology of Masonic symbols, including the well-known image of crossed compasses and square.

The large plate was made around 1820 for Sir Walter Scott; the crest that appears on the rim—a lady with outstretched arms—formed part of the Scott family's coat of arms. The saucer, whose lion crest is unidentified, has a similar border and may have been made in the same Chinese workshop.

The Rich China Trade

An ivory box, intricately carved with a floral relief, was a lady's needle case, part of a fancy sewing set made for export about 1800.

O n Sunday last sailed from New York, the ship *Empress of China* for Canton in China," announced a local paper in 1784. "The Captain and crew were all elated on being considered the first instruments, in the hands of Providence, who have undertaken to extend the commerce of the United States to that distant, and to us unexplored, country."

By the 1820s about 30 to 40 American ships a year were entering the Canton harbor, unloading American ginseng, furs and silver coins and taking on tea, silk and export porcelain.

The trade involved high risks and adventure, especially for the super-cargoes—American importers' representatives who went along with the ships on their yearlong voyages. Business was rigidly supervised by agents of the Manchu rulers, who feared their institutions were threatened by "foreign devils." Western merchants were confined to a ¼-mile-long section of the waterfront, where they lived and traded only with licensed hongs and their compradors, or contact men. The visitors could not bring women with them, carry weapons or even go rowing unsupervised.

Nevertheless, many young Americans found China fascinating and, along with the goods they bought for their employers, shopped privately for what one captain called "the little elegancies of life," like those shown. While not as common as export porcelain, they too tempt collectors.

This silver tea caddy was made in Shanghai for a visiting Yankee in 1855. It is fitted with a lock to protect its costly contents.

This embroidered silk mandarin square was designed for the back of a government official's robe. According to canons of 19th Century Chinese court dress, a crane identified the wearer as holding the highest civilian rank in the bureaucracy, First Degree Mandarin.

Popular souvenirs among returning Western merchants and sailors were waterfront views such as this one of Hong Kong by an anonymous Chinese artist. It shows a harbor crowded with foreign ships come to trade after the port opened in 1841. The high, ungainly ship at left center is a floating warehouse where English traders stored goods while waiting for ships to carry them home.

Labels like this, called tea facings, were pasted on shipping crates of tea to identify the contents. This facing, block-printed by hand on rice paper, ungrammatically touts Great Mogul tea as "extra choicest."

One of the select compradors licensed to trade with the West, Mougua was a Cantonese of wealth and power when this portrait was done in 1835 by a Chinese artist imitating Western painting techniques.

An unusually large Rose Medallion piece, made about 1800, has six scenes of figures in landscapes encircling a central medallion with a favorite theme of Chinese painting— birds and butterflies among trees and rocks.

Two similar Rose Medallion plates, each with white areas, or reserves, demonstrate some differences in quality and workmanship. The valuable 1840 plate on the left, monogrammed and thus made to order, bears fine painting, subtle colorations and a nice esthetic balance between reserves and background. The undated plate at right, much less valuable, suffers from oversized reserves, harsh colors and coarse technique.

The soup tureen at left utilizes designs characteristic of Rose Medallion, but the placement typical of plates and bowls is rearranged. The medallion, usually in the center of the piece, is replaced by a finial and is moved to the side.

An accessory dish for a family service, this small leaf-shaped tray probably served as a rest for a ladle. It was painted in the Mandarin style about 1840 in emulation of 18th Century classical Chinese painting.

This covered sugar bowl, in a style called Rose Canton, was made in 1840. Although it was most likely a stock piece, it is distinguished for its graceful contours, handsome strap handles and a gilt strawberry finial.

Chinese courtesans disport in an idealized garden on a shell-shaped serving dish. The monochromatic rendition of the Mandarin-style figures makes this dish an unusual find.

The Mandarin serving dish and lid below were made for a British church society. Hot water was poured into the double-walled dish through the spout at left to keep food warm.

This bowl, made around 1870, is an eclectic combination of Rose Canton motifs on the body and a border in the style collectors call Hundred Butterflies. Butterflies symbolized, among other things, wedded bliss.

The Blue Trellis border that rims this scallop-edged bowl provides the key to dating the piece. This design came into fashion on Rose Medallion porcelain toward the end of the export trade, in the late 19th Century.

A lady attended by joyful servants provides the theme for a Mandarin plate of 1815. Though the illustration is similar to many others, the orange rim is unusual, making this piece a collector's rarity.

The Manchu court—a meeting place of scholars and beautiful princesses—is depicted on an 1810 Mandarin plate. The artist dispensed with the usual formal border to use the entire surface for illustration.

This monogrammed piece uses as decorations symbols drawn from the Chinese religion of Taoism. The female figure above the monogram, for example, represents one of the eight Taoist Immortals.

Ornamented in the complex Hundred Butterflies style with a very fine gold and green bordering, the dish above is shaped like a stylized scallop shell, a form long popular in the West.

The final stage in the development of the Hundred Butterflies pattern was reached about 1860, when this lozenge-shaped bowl was made. Dozens of butterflies decorate the white spaces on the bowl, as well as the ornate and heavily gilded parts of the border.

This close-up of a yellow-ocher covered dish reveals the meticulous brushwork and fine shading of the best Chinese export ware.

This pair of 4-inch-high elephant figures might have served equally well for export or domestic markets: the holders on the animals' backs were originally incense burners, but in the West they conveniently became *candleholders. Elephants were a popular form for such pieces, recalling to Chinese the beast that bore the sacred jewels of Buddha, but artisans also favored the cock, duck, deer and a variety of dog breeds.*

MUSEUMS

The Art Institute of Chicago
Chicago, Illinois 60603

Henry Francis du Pont Winterthur Museum
Winterthur, Delaware 19735

The Metropolitan Museum of Art
New York, New York 10028

Museum of the American China Trade
Milton, Massachusetts 02186

Museum of Fine Arts
Boston, Massachusetts 02115

Peabody Museum of Salem
Salem, Massachusetts 01970

Philadelphia Museum of Art
Philadelphia, Pennsylvania 19101

Western Reserve Historical Society and
Frederick C. Crawford Auto-Aviation Museum
Cleveland, Ohio 44106

BOOKS
Gordon, Elinor:
Collecting Chinese Export Porcelain. Universe Books, 1977.
Chinese Export Porcelain: An Historical Survey. Universe Books, 1977.

Howard, David S.:
Chinese Armorial Porcelain. Faber & Faber, 1974.
China for the West, 2 vols. Sotheby Bernet, 1978.

Hyde, J. A. Lloyd, *Oriental Lowestoft.* The Ceramic Book Co., 1964.

Le Corbeiller, Clare, *China Trade Porcelain: Patterns of Exchange.* The Metropolitan Museum of Art, 1974.

Mudge, Jean McClure, *Chinese Export Porcelain for the American Trade, 1785 to 1835.* University of Delaware Press, 1967.

Palmer, Arlene M., *A Winterthur Guide to Chinese Export Porcelain.* Crown Publishers, Inc., 1976.

Phillips, John Goldsmith, *China Trade Porcelain.* Harvard University Press, 1956.

Scheurleer, D. F. Lunsingh, *Chinese Export Porcelain: Chine de Commande.* Pitman Publishing Corp., 1974.

Williamson, George C., *The Book of Famille Rose.* Chas. E. Tuttle Company, 1970.

Christmas Tree Ornaments
Reminders of a Festive Season

This 2-inch-high Victorian house, of embossed cardboard with candy-box lace for eaves, was made in Dresden, Germany, around 1900.

Back in the 1950s when I wandered into antique stores in hopes of finding old Christmas tree ornaments, the dealers appeared amused. "Nobody asks for them," they would say. Today the responses are completely different. "You're the fifth person this month to ask me for them," one man said to me. "What is it with old Christmas tree ornaments?"

There are two answers. One is simply the nostalgia we feel for an old-fashioned Christmas. The other is more complicated. People are beginning to appreciate anew the artistry that went into the making of the various little figures and objects that decorated Christmas trees around the turn of the century.

Store-bought tree ornaments were introduced around 1870 to replace homemade—generally edible—decorations. Most of them came from Germany, from Dresden and tiny villages in the Thuringian Mountains, where a tradition of cottage craftsmanship had existed for centuries. The ornaments came in several forms. The earliest

Phillip Snyder, an advertising art director, finds in collecting Christmas tree ornaments the wonderment he felt in yuletide celebrations as a child.

versions were flat geometric shapes, such as stars and crosses, made of lead, like toy soldiers. Later versions were of wax, like the angel and swinging children on page 45, or of cotton wool that was folded and glued over wire or cardboard frames, like the three examples at left. These cotton-wool ornaments, decorated with embossed paper faces and such details as buttons, powdered glass and gold paper wings, were often children's favorites—probably because they were unbreakable and therefore were the only tree ornaments children were allowed to play with.

My own favorites are a kind of embossed, three-

A gold-winged angel and two versions of Father Christmas, all of which were sculpted by hand of cotton wool around the turn of the century, sparkle under their coatings of powdered glass.

dimensional cardboard ornaments made in Dresden between 1880 and 1910. Most—like the tiny house on page 40—are covered with gold or silver paper, but a few are hand-painted. They were available in a variety of shapes that appears infinite—polar bears, camels, storks, peacocks, miniature bicycles, skates, sleds, locomotives, ships, pianos—and they are marvelous examples of painstaking workmanship. Every one of the ornaments was stamped and cut in several parts, then turned over to cottage workers for assembly. An elephant formed from two halves that were glued together had a howdah with curtains made of real silk attached to its back *(page 37);* violins were strung with silk thread; a steamboat, 2 inches long, was equipped with a movable rudder and turning paddle wheel.

I first came across a collection of these miniature Dresden ornaments one Christmas displayed in the window of a shop that was just off Rittenhouse Square in Philadelphia. The ornaments belonged to the owner of the shop and were not for sale, but I started acquiring others wherever I could find them. And I did not forget my Rittenhouse Square inspiration. Every year during the Christmas season I made a pilgrimage to the shop—in the hope that the shop owner's ornaments might someday be offered for sale. Then one Christmas they were gone; the owner had died.

It took me an entire year to track down these Dresden ornaments; I finally found them in another antique shop outside Philadelphia. I dialed the phone number I had been given, and a voice at the other end of the line said that, yes, the ornaments had been in his possession, but that he no longer had them. "You may remember that we had a flood in this area after Hurricane Agnes," he said. When he opened his flood-ruined shop the morning after the storm had hit, a single gold cardboard carriage wheel had come floating toward him across the muddy water. It had been part of a tiny replica of a coronation coach, and it was all that remained from the

These tiny cardboard shoes have drawstring silk tops and were filled with candy and hung on the tree. The shoe at bottom right is velvet covered.

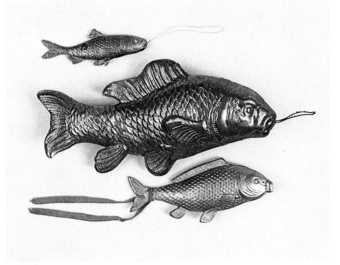

The Christmas carp, a European tradition, inspired these gold and silver cardboard fish. The largest is 6 inches long, the smallest 2 inches.

Rittenhouse Square collection. So I dejectedly closed my books on the case.

The Dresden ornaments are so scarce that the majority of antique dealers have never even seen one. This is peculiar in a way, because the cardboard from which they are made is surprisingly resistant to the ravages of time and generations of handling. Perhaps the Dresden pieces are rare because by the turn of the century the majority of the earlier forms of Christmas tree decorations had been superseded by the blown-glass ornaments that have ever since been considered a part of the American Christmas tree.

In the 1870s, when blown-glass ornaments first went on sale in the United States, no one would have been able to predict their extraordinary success. In the fall of 1880 they were offered to a young dime-store merchant named Frank Woolworth by a German importer. Woolworth thought the ornaments were foolish, and told the importer so. Still, many of the customers of his store, which was in Lancaster, Pennsylvania, were of German descent, and decorated Christmas trees were a strong German tradition. So Woolworth purchased $25 worth. "In two days," he later recalled, "they were gone, and I woke up." Within 10 years his annual order was for some 200,000 blown-glass ornaments, and Woolworth, who was by then the owner of 14 stores, was visiting the village of Lauscha, where the ornaments were made, to place his order in person.

Lauscha, in the Thuringian Mountains, has been a center for glassmaking since the 16th Century, when a group of Protestant glass blowers relocated there from Swabia, now a part of Bavaria, in order to escape religious persecution. To entertain themselves, the Lauscha craftsmen frequently blew glass balls to see how large

they could make them. By the 1820s the artisans were silvering the inside of the balls with lead or zinc and using them for household decorations. Soon the balls were being used for decorating Christmas trees, and in 1848 the first known order for *Weihnachtsbaum Kugeln*—Christmas tree balls—appeared in a Lauscha glass blower's order book.

In 1857 Louis Greiner-Schlotfeger, one of the Lauscha glassmakers, developed the formula for silvering that has ever since given Christmas tree ornaments their characteristic, mirror-like shine. Greiner-Schlotfeger—who might be referred to as the Thomas Edison of Christmas tree ornaments—also perfected a modification of the *Kugel* that was paper-thin. He also has been credited with the development of the first ornament made of molded glass, which he is said to have created by blowing a glass bubble directly into a wooden cookie mold shaped like a pine cone.

Assisted by Greiner-Schlotfeger's improvements, the Lauscha glass-blowing industry started to flourish. Before long it involved everyone in the village. The men were responsible for blowing the glass; the women did the silvering; the children applied the lacquer and paint and added the caps. By 1889 Christmas tree ornaments were the most important product of the village, and American importers such as Woolworth were making side trips to Lauscha on a regular basis from Nuremberg, which was 60 miles away, when they traveled to Germany to shop for dolls and toys.

With decades of expertise behind them, the German glass blowers by 1900 were producing not just Christmas tree balls but all sorts of sculptured ornaments as well. These included fruits and vegetables, fish and fowl, animals, storybook characters, and a whole range of novelty

A steam engine with a cotton puff of smoke and an elephant with a silk-curtained howdah are among this array of cardboard modes of transportation.

Animals of every kind, wild and domestic, were a favorite subject of the Dresden artisans who made cardboard ornaments until about the turn of the century. Most were simply gilded and silvered, making the realistically painted household pets above rare as well as charming.

Light-Bulb Ornaments

Although 19th Century tree decorations have been important as collectibles only since the mid-1970s, many people have had a long fascination with the sculptured light bulbs that adorned American trees in the 1920s and 1930s. For that reason, they are found in antique shops more often than are other Christmas decorations.

The first of these bulbs were made and painted by hand in Vienna just after the turn of the century, when the electric light was a relatively new invention. They were delicate pieces of work in the shape of flowers, fruits, birds and animals, and were imperfectly copied by both American and Japanese craftsmen. The copies too were made by hand, but by 1919 machine-made bulbs were being produced in the United States by General Electric in a variety of shapes, including stars, tulips and Santas.

The Japanese bulbs continued to be handmade until around World War II, but their glass was heavier and the workmanship cruder than that of the originals from Vienna. Their paint became chipped and cracked; around 1917 the Japanese began switching from clear glass to milk glass so that these flaws would be less visible.

Eventually the Japanese not only copied the Austrian originals, but also created replicas of various American cartoon characters, such as Little Orphan Annie and Andy Gump. The Oriental flavor of their work is subtle but unmistakable: many of the Japanese Santa Claus bulbs look as much like Buddha as Saint Nick.

A minstrel and a rosebud (above) are rare examples of the hand-painted tree bulbs made in Vienna between 1900 and 1917.

Japanese Christmas tree lights—some in the shape of comic-strip characters—delighted American children from the 1920s to the 1950s.

A glass snowman is shown with the plaster-of-paris mold in which it was blown by German craftsmen in the village of Lauscha. Between the 1880s and the 1930s, the Lauscha glass blowers produced thousands of molds, which collectors value as highly as the ornaments made in them.

items, such as pocket watches, baby carriages and pipes. By the 1920s their repertoire included, at the request of American customers, such technological marvels as automobiles and airplanes. No one knows for certain the number of different designs that were produced over the years, but a conservative estimate places the figure at approximately 5,000. This presents wonderful opportunities to ornament collectors, but unfortunately it also creates some problems.

Ornaments are valued for their age and rarity, but these particular characteristics can be very difficult to determine. Some of the designs were produced for only a single season by a single glass blower—and, of course, such pieces are rare. But other designs were produced for five decades or longer. I am always wary of any dealer who guarantees the antiquity of an ornament, since the molds can be used over and over again, and a quite recent piece can come out of a venerable mold. In addition, no matter what the original production figures were, ornaments from the 19th Century tend to be in short supply. Chemical imbalances in much of the glass that was used then cause the ornaments to self-destruct eventually. And cats' paws, dogs' tails and children's elbows have also taken their toll.

The antiquity of one kind of ornament, the original *Kugel,* as it was made before Greiner-Schlotfeger's improvements, can be guaranteed. The *Kugeln* are immediately identified by their thick glass and dull sheen. They made their first appearance in America in the 1860s, mixed in with the household treasures of immigrants from Germany. Because their heavy construction made the ornaments sufficiently sturdy to withstand accidents, many of them survived and can still be discovered in attics and antique shops. And since they were no longer produced after the turn of the century, a *Kugel* is

definitely a product of the 19th Century—though beyond that, dating is speculative.

Perhaps the most reliable indications of age in a glass ornament are to be found in its design and construction, and in the mellowing process. Any glass ball that is decorated with wire tinsel, cotton batting or silk tassels is very likely to have been made between about 1890 and 1910, when designs such as these were popular. And if you come across an ornament whose top is finished with a round metal cap pierced by a hole, it almost certainly predates World War I. Before the appearance of the spring-clip fastener commonly used today, many ornaments were fastened to the tree with a piece of string that was passed through the hole in these rounded caps. Other fastening devices found on ornaments from this period include glass hooks that are integral parts of the ornament, and metal spring clamps such as those used for Christmas tree candles.

Patina as a sign of age is perhaps the most certain method of determining the date of an ornament's manufacture. In the very oldest pieces, both the lacquered surface and the silvered lining are softly mellowed. In addition, you may find that the silvering is cracked, similar to the silvering that backs an old mirror. Sometimes this cracking occurs in a pattern of horizontal rings, although ring cracks are not to be considered an infallible sign of age; they also are found in some improperly silvered post-World War II ornaments.

As the value of Christmas tree ornaments escalates, they paradoxically become easier for collectors to find. Dealers buying estates now consider it well worth their while to hold on to objects that they would formerly have discarded as being too fragile to bother with. And owners wishing to sell their ornaments now find it advantageous to advertise them in the classified columns of collectors' magazines. However, if you plan to purchase ornaments through the mail, be sure to ask the seller to wrap them carefully in tissue paper, pack them in metal cookie or coffee cans and place the containers inside corrugated boxes. Also, caution the seller not to attempt to wash his ornaments. Any sort of water or dampness will cause the lacquer on an old ornament to peel right off; they should never be cleaned with anything except a soft, dry cloth.

Lest these precautionary measures make it sound as though collecting Christmas tree ornaments is a pastime meant only for brain surgeons, let me hasten to add that my own ornament collection is in use every single year. It seems somehow alien to the spirit of Christmas to lock away even admittedly fragile ornaments from the hands of children, when a little common sense and discretion can keep these valuable items perfectly intact. The appropriate place for Christmas tree ornaments is, after all, on a Christmas tree.

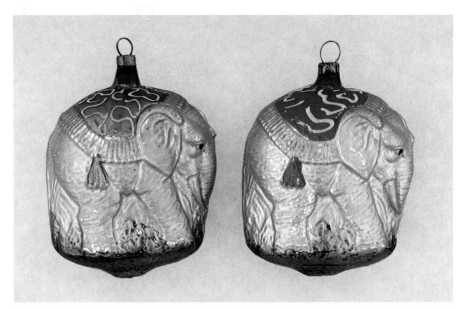

Buildings of all kinds, from cottages (above) to churches, are popular Lauscha glass designs.

Although these glass elephants were blown from the same mold, they were painted differently; the ring hanging device indicates that they are from the 1920s.

Fruits, nuts and vegetables produced by the Lauscha craftsmen come in various sizes. The corn above is 3 ½ inches long; the walnut, 1 ¼ inches long.

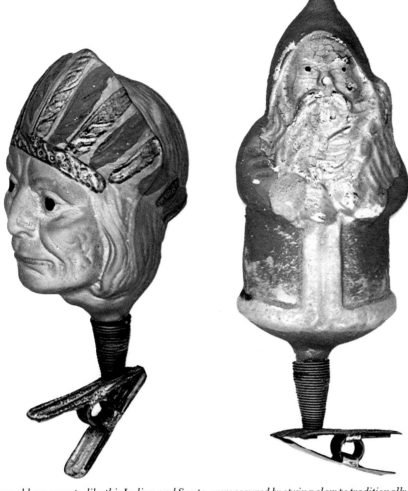

Many old ornaments, like this Indian and Santa, were secured by spring clamps traditionally used in Germany to hold Christmas tree candles. Such ornaments are rare today.

This lacquered blue dog is one of many canines in different colors made from the same mold.

Three faces, including a whimsical one on a pear, illustrate the kind of intricate modeling for which Lauscha tree ornaments are noted by collectors.

This free-blown coffeepot, made without a mold, required enormous expertise to shape. The delicate spout and handle were made separately.

In the early years of this century, free-blown ornaments, like the three above, were often painted with glue, then sprinkled with crushed glass.

Delicate trumpets twisted from molten straws of glass were among the most difficult of the ornaments that were fashioned by the German artisans.

Paper sails and flags and strands of crinkled wire tinsel decorate these three imaginative airship ornaments from Germany.

To satisfy the tastes of the Victorian era, these turn-of-the-century ornaments were embellished with wire, velvet, cotton wool, tinsel and silk tassels.

Antique Tree Stands

These two antique cast-iron tree stands on tripod bases were meant to be screwed to a wooden support for greater stability.

Christmas trees have been held up by structures that were as simple as home-carpentered tripods and buckets of coal. But during the 19th Century a number of ingenious inventions were patented for supporting the tree in style. The first American patents for Christmas tree stands were issued in 1876 to two Philadelphians, Abram C. Mott and Hermann Albrecht. Albrecht later patented an improved design, which used a cylindrical socket to receive the tree and an encircling ring to steady it; when the ring was turned, it moved three clamps against the trunk *(above, right)*. Like its predecessors, the stand had three feet and looked not unlike the cast-iron stands then used for flagpoles—a use that Mott and Albrecht noted in their patent applications.

Other devices for anchoring included a double-pronged arrangement patented in 1891 by Martin Merk *(above, left)*, which bracketed the tree trunk and was fastened against it by a screw nut under the trivet-like base. For collectors, one virtue of Merk's design is that his name and the date of his patent are inscribed on the rim of the base, making it very easy for the stand to be identified.

But not all Christmas tree stands were strictly functional. Among the 20 or more that received patents before the close of the century was one, patented in 1878 by Johannes C. Eckardt, that featured a spring-wound mechanism for revolving the tree, and a music box that played a Christmas tune. And in 1899 an inventor named Alfred Wagner came up with a stand that not only made the tree revolve with an electric motor but also preserved its freshness by keeping its base submerged in water.

Lead-alloy tree ornaments like these, faceted like jewels, were first made in Germany in the late 1700s and are among the oldest made for sale.

Homemade paper cornucopias full of candies, dried fruits, popcorn and nuts hung on many Victorian Christmas trees; now they are quite rare.

Wax ornaments like the two swinging children at right adorned many Christmas trees from the 1870s to the 1890s; wax angels like the one above were popular into the 1930s.

In the 1890s mail-order firms like Sears, Roebuck touted tinsel ornaments as more durable than "old style German glass tree ornaments."

MUSEUMS AND LIBRARIES
Seasonal exhibits of Christmas tree ornaments:

The Henry Ford Museum and Greenfield Village
Dearborn, Michigan 48121

The Henry Francis duPont Winterthur Museum
Winterthur, Delaware 19735

Smithsonian Institution
Washington, D.C. 21560

PERIODICALS
The Antique Trader, Babka Publishing Company,
Inc., Dubuque, Iowa 52001

BOOKS
Foley, Daniel J., *The Christmas Tree.* Chilton
Company, 1960.

Rogers, Maggie, with Judith Hawkins, *The Glass
Christmas Ornament: Old and New.* Timber Press,
1977.

Snyder, Phillip V., *The Christmas Tree Book.* The Viking
Press, 1976.

Cigar Bands and Labels
Pop Art from a Smoke

Like many other collectors, the aficionados of cigar bands and labels have a favorite story about a fake. But their story is unique in a number of respects, not least because the fake is a magazine clipping. The February 1933 issue of FORTUNE ran a report on the cigar business with full-sized pictures of 20 cigar bands. Most were common, made by the millions with such familiar brand names as White Owl, Admiration and El Producto, but one was in great demand among collectors. It bore the trademarks of Coca-Cola, one of many designs prepared for that company between 1927 and 1944 for cigars handed out at sales conventions.

As time passed, the value of a real Coca-Cola band—nearly all had been crushed into ashtrays—increased to

---

Norman Waltz works for a battery manufacturer in the cigar-making area of Lancaster County, Pennsylvania.

$100 or more. And old copies of that 1933 FORTUNE became a gold mine for the fakers. For the FORTUNE illustration is almost identical to the genuine band, partly because it was full-sized but also because it was a "tip-in," specially printed on one side only on cigar-band paper from cigar-band plates (10 colors plus metallic gold), by a lithography company that specialized in cigar bands. In this sense the illustration was not a copy but a true cigar band, even though it never was meant to be wrapped around a cigar. A hand skilled with a razor blade could cut it out of the tip-in and pass it off as the real thing. However, the FORTUNE illustration differs from most Coca-Cola bands in a way that a knowledgeable collector can spot. The illustration had been printed from a plate that shows the familiar curved bottle turned at an angle. This plate was apparently used only briefly, then discarded in favor of a head-on view of the bottle *(page 49)*, and most of the cigars actually given away from 1927 to 1944 bore the later version.

Special-purpose bands like Coca-Cola's are particularly desirable—even the fake is valued for its notoriety—

This unusual fan-shaped cigar box, dating from the turn of the century, holds a 70-year-old cigar; the original band, which ordinarily would be removed from the cigar for preservation, is still in place. Another Radiana box label, never used, is at left.

because they are printed in relatively small numbers and thus are scarce. But many others are also prized, as are the garish and often amusing labels used on cigar boxes.

Collecting cigar bands and labels began soon after the collectibles became items of commerce. Europeans had smoked cigars since the 16th Century; early explorers introduced the habit after they had observed Indians smoking tobacco rolled inside dried palm or corn leaves. But no one provided bands or decorated boxes with fancy labels until the middle of the 19th Century.

Why the bands were put on cigars in the first place is something of a mystery. One idea is that Cuban ladies, who smoked cigars long before using tobacco became acceptable among women of other countries, picked up their cigars with strips of paper to prevent nicotine stains on their fingers. Others suggest that English dandies began the practice to protect their fashionable white gloves. Or perhaps the famed cigar maker Gustave Bock, whose name identified good cigars for more than a century, invented them. He claimed that in 1854, annoyed by inferior cigars being sold as his, he had bands printed to protect his fine brand.

At any rate, sometime in the 1850s and 1860s, manufacturers realized that decorative cigar bands and box labels could be used to great advantage. They vied with one another by having their printers commission artists to come up with florid, eye-catching designs of lush tobacco plants, beautiful women and romantic moonlight scenes. Up to 22 colors, each requiring a separate press-run, were used for a label. Bronzing powder, fancy silk- or satin-finished papers and elaborate embossing gussied up many examples. An 1888 New York *Sun* article remarked that the "label is often better than the cigar."

The *Sun*'s comment may explain why people began to collect these outlandish examples of 19th Century advertising kitsch. Around the turn of the century, bands in particular were saved, presumably by women, to be glued to the undersides of glass ashtrays. Others pasted them in scrapbooks. The avocation enlisted well-known personages, a number of whom happened to be writers: Rex Beach; George Bernard Shaw, who once asked his American lawyer to get him a complete set of bands printed in the United States; and Ernest Hemingway, who supposedly gave Ava Gardner a cigar band as a sou-

Brand names on box labels had to be printed in letters that were big, brassy and distinctive enough to catch a customer's attention amid a clutter of similarly flamboyant attractions inside a glass-topped cigar counter. The design at top is a peculiar combination of turn-of-the-century Art Nouveau and imaginary Oriental touches, while the one at left includes ornamental curlicues. The two at bottom attempt to suggest the product or the brand name, with cigar-like shading inside the letters at left and a breezy seascape at right.

venir of their first meeting (there is no record that she collected more). My introduction to cigar memorabilia came in 1965 when an 80-year-old neighbor, who had collected since he was a boy, gave me about 600 early bands. In the next 10 years or so I added 27,000 more.

During the first decades of the 20th Century, the hobby created such demand that printers sold unused bands directly to collectors. Some of these bands were patriotic: at least 13 Presidential sets—picturing the 25 Presidents from Washington through Theodore Roosevelt—were issued by competing companies; they are quite valuable today. For $1.25 in the 1920s you could buy a mint-condition Presidential set that had never touched cigars. Also there are sets depicting 24 tribes of Indians, a uniquely American subject printed in Europe for export—one set in Holland, one in Belgium.

Many collectors pursue a personal interest, looking for memorabilia of airplanes and dirigibles (page 53), or Wild West heroes (page 51). Others specialize in rare bands with pictures of politicians who tried to get votes by passing out cigars during campaigns. Particularly prized are outsized bands—my biggest is 3½ inches by 18 inches—that secured bundles of cigars.

Older material is more valuable than newer—a band or label of the period between 1870 and 1930, when cigar smoking declined, is especially desirable—but the decoration or brand name may give it value. The rich and famous (and some not so rich or famous) ordered personalized cigars: Rudyard Kipling, a nonstop smoker, had "R. K." embossed on his bands and box labels. Many clubs and restaurants and nearly all cigar stores have had private brands, marked with names and insignia as are book matches and cocktail napkins.

Commercial brand names are as desirable as private ones because so many of them were zanily inappropriate: Bank Note, Dividend Payer, Round Up, Rocky Road, Omar (page 48), The Strawberry (page 52), Optic (page 56). Nearly all have long disappeared from cigar counters, but once they were numerous: 350,000 brands in 1900. And even modern ones have interesting histories: for example, La Palina tried to give a Cuban aura to cigars made in Chicago by Sam Paley (a picture of Mrs. Paley in Spanish costume adorns the box).

Bands and labels of cigars still on the market intrigue many collectors, who attempt to acquire complete historical sets tracing design modifications, many of them subtle. For example, many White Owl bands have series numbers and letters in the left-hand edge. I enjoy assembling the "A" and "B" series in numerical sequence. I also have 80 variations of Phillies bands from the 1970s, when that Philadelphia company began using about 120 slightly different bands for its many varieties of sizes and tobacco types.

Box labels are scarcer than bands but are often more

Among sought-after bands is the Buster Brown at bottom. It was designed by Richard Outcault, who created the character for a comic strip—one of the first—and then sold the right to use the name and picture on products from shoes to cigars. The Smiles band at top identified cigars distributed by the now-defunct Southern Grocery Company.

During the years from 1927 to 1944 the Coca-Cola Company used bands on cigars that were given away at company meetings. Genuine Coca-Cola bands, like the top two, are so valuable that even a fake—a magazine clipping (bottom) that can be detected by the angle of the bottle in the picture—is considered desirable.

The four bands above are prized because of their pictures. From the top, they depict radio and screen personality Eddie Cantor, a fire chief, an Indian and the cigar-making Tinkham brothers.

rewarding, chiefly because the larger size allowed artists to express their fancies. Label size varies: 4-inch squares are rarer than the 6-inch rectangles also used on box lids; apparently the larger were more popular with manufacturers. Oblong labels used on the sides were usually simple, as were labels on the outside top—called "outs" to distinguish them from the fancier "ins."

Since boxes are so bulky, most collectors remove labels by soaking them in cool water until the glue softens and they float off. They may be dried flat in a book of blotter paper such as photographers use. Then they, and the bands, can be mounted in scrapbooks with the removable gummed-paper hinges favored by stamp collectors.

Hunting for these artifacts is fascinating because success may depend on a knowledge of turn-of-the-century social and industrial history. The bands and labels have been saved for so long that old collections are likely to turn up in the usual places—attics, auctions, flea markets and particularly antique shops specializing in what is called paper ephemera. Once at a flea market I got 2,000 bands for $75, including three Coca-Cola bands—

These three turn-of-the-century portrait labels show the poet Henry Wadsworth Longfellow, a dream-girl creation of the illustrator Howard Chandler Christy, and another favorite poet, Walt Whitman.

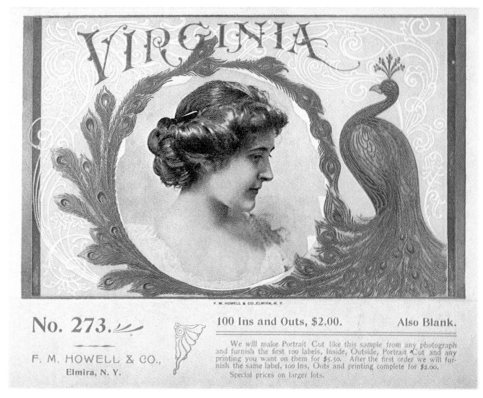

Smokers who wanted personalized boxes for gifts could have a photograph of wife or sweetheart printed on a label that could be chosen from a catalogue like the one above. A flat charge is listed for "ins and outs"—labels for the inside and outside of a box—and the full costs are quoted underneath.

two genuine ones and one the fake from FORTUNE.

The most fertile hunting grounds are around cigar-making centers. Big ones were strung along the East Coast: Philadelphia, New York and their satellites, such as Trenton and Jersey City, New Jersey. Others were in tobacco-growing areas: the Connecticut River valley, where the special leaf for cigar wrappers is cultivated; my home county of Lancaster, in the midst of Pennsylvania's tobacco farms; and Richmond and the North Carolina cities in the old tobacco country. Tampa, Florida, is a special place—less than 400 miles from Cuba, it was the home of bonded factories that made cigars from Cuban tobacco; the boxes bear a government stamp certifying that only Cuban tobacco was used, and some boxes are marked with the Tampa city seal.

Printers who were in business nearby in the old days —especially those who did color lithography—are a source to consider; their names and addresses might be found in small type in the lower left margin of a lid label. Using these potential mines of material poses special problems. Since few present-day printers will let you poke through their storerooms—many will not even answer letters from collectors—you must be alert for the occasional opportunity to find out what they may have. Company histories can give a clue to work done in the past. And if a plant moves, is taken over or closes, you may get a chance to participate in the clean-up process. Best of all—at least for collectors—is an auction disposing of a firm's assets when it goes out of business.

The cigar industry was not concentrated solely in a few areas around 1900. Every tank town and whistle stop had a cigar store with its own brand, specially ordered from a big company or made locally by a small one. Before World War I, cigar makers, many employing only two or three workers, operated in almost every city and in small factory towns across the country, from Norwich, New York, to Belle Fontaine, Ohio. Relics of their products can still be found if you are willing to do some research. By checking old newspapers for the names of the proprietors of cigar stores, factories and printers, then tracing through church and vital-statistic records for descendants, you may track them down by phone. If you find someone who is willing to part with family souvenirs, you will have made a rare find—but if the souvenirs include actual cigars, remove the bands at once. The tobacco may attract the tobacco beetle, whose tiny larvae eat holes in the paper bands.

For related material, see the article on Fruit Crate Labels in a separate volume of this encyclopedia.

*This seldom-found label for The Strawberry cigar, with a fanci-
ful fairy-tale picture that was copyrighted in 1874, is the oldest
label in the author's collection. The initials of the cigar maker,
Fred Wambach, can be seen on the carriage.*

The name on this gold-embossed label captioned the picture for 19th Century smokers: wheelers were the strongest draft animals in a team, the pair positioned directly ahead of the front wheels of a wagon.

Many collectors group labels by themes, such as transport. The Spirit of St. Louis marks Lindbergh's historic 1927 flight; the lower label uses the ubiquitous taxicab company's name. Both are labels for the ends of boxes.

Pictures of dogs, cats or horses might be expected on cigar labels, but the appeal of a creature like the crab is somewhat less understandable—and the label is rare.

The German airships called zeppelins inspired this inside-lid label. But it shows the American dirigible "Los Angeles" flying from Friedrichshafen, Germany, to the Lakehurst, New Jersey, base near New York.

*The seal (top) that held the box closed, the box label (center) and side label
(bottom) of this set depict Chief Justice Salmon Chase (he was Governor
of Ohio in the late 1850s, although the labels are much more recent).*

The large band (top), 5½ inches by 2½ inches, with a portrait of President Wilson, was wrapped in many layers around one cigar. The smaller bands, which bear the likenesses of Presidents Washington and John Adams, were never used; they were included in a Presidential set of

25. The large label below, which was reproduced from a printer's catalogue, was available to help promote the candidacies of Alton Parker and Henry Davis, the Democratic nominees for President and Vice President who lost the election of 1904.

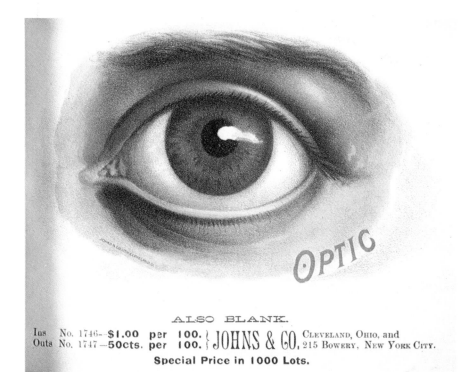

ALSO BLANK.

Ins   No. 1746—$1.00 per 100. } JOHNS & CO, Cleveland, Ohio, and
Outs No. 1747—50cts. per 100.   215 Bowery, New York City.
Special Price in 1000 Lots.

Whether the brand name and staring image of the label at top had anything to do with the medical or optical profession is conjectural. It is reproduced from the catalogue of a printer who charged more for the large "ins" than for the smaller "outs." Our Prescription (bottom), amplified in a coy text, is undoubtedly that of the cigar manufacturer, not of a physician.

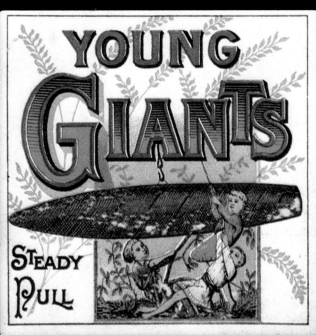

The four labels above demonstrate the imaginative way in which cigars and designs were used together to illustrate brand identification. The price printed on the upper-right-hand label doubled as the brand name, and the two at the bottom include typical puns.

The Dating of Cigar Labels

Only in rare instances will a date appear on a cigar label or band, in a copyright notice or hidden in the design. But clues can be found in printing technique and subject matter. Zeppelins, for example, cannot appear before 1900, when the first one flew. And style or a signature may identify an artist whose working years are known *(opposite)*.

A rough division between old and recent material can be achieved by determining the system of printing. All labels that were made before 1900 and many after that date were printed in a variety of colors by the old-fashioned lithography method; its irregular, coarse strokes, made by a craftsman's crayon on the lithographic "stone" are revealed by close observation *(below, right)*. Around the turn of the century, printers started to use photolithography, which broke the image into tiny dots of colors *(bottom, right)*. However, for several decades both processes were used. Paper also provides evidence of age—prior to 1880 cigar labels and bands were printed on smooth, thin paper without gold leaf or heavy embossing.

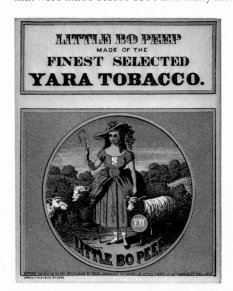

These labels illustrate differences in the method of printing that help establish their age. Little Bo Peep is old-fashioned color lithography, which requires a craftsman's textured crayon strokes, visible in the enlargement (above, right). The Whale-Back label below was done by the photomechanical process that took over completely after 1930, shown by the evenly spaced dots in the magnified detail.

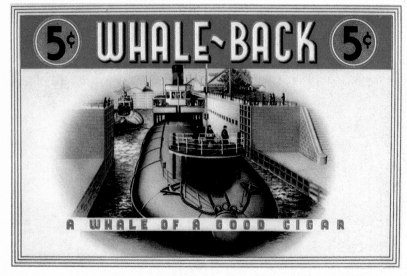

The work of well-known artists often appeared on cigar-box labels. This picture is by cartoonist Eugene Zimmerman, called Zim, and is identifi- *able by his characters, who wore patched clothes and oversized shoes. Since Zim was famous in the late 1890s, the picture helps date this label.*

MUSEUMS AND LIBRARIES
The Metropolitan Museum of Art
The Burdick Collection
New York, New York 10028

Museum of the City of New York
New York, New York 10029

National Tobacco-Textile Museum
Danville, Virginia 24541

The New York Public Library
The Arents Collection
New York, New York 10018

COLLECTORS ORGANIZATIONS
International Seal, Label & Cigar Band Society
8915 East Bellevue Street

Tucson, Arizona 85715

BOOKS
Back, J. B., *The Pleasures of Cigar Smoking.* Rutledge Books, Inc., 1971.

Davidoff, Zino, *The Connoisseur's Book of the Cigar.* McGraw-Hill Book Company, 1969.

Faber, A. D., *Cigar Label Art.* Century House, 1949.

Hyman, H. Tony, *Handbook of American Cigar Boxes.* Arnot Art Museum, 235 Lake Street, Elmira, New York 14801, 1978.

Scott, Amoret and Christopher, *Tobacco and the Collector.* Max Parrish and Co., Ltd., 1966.

P.T. BARNUM'S GREATEST SHOW ON EARTH,

TRAVELING THIS SEASON ONLY — UNITED — ACTUA

MIRRORE

CHARIOT — GOLDEN ERA.

LEADING THE FIRST GRAND DIVISION OF THE GR

SANGER'S ROYAL BRITISH MENAGERIE AND GRAND I

4 A COMBINATION OF THE LARGEST SHOWS. — P.T. BARNUM, J.A. BAILEY & J.L. HU

SOLE OWNERS.

Circus Memorabilia
Echoes of the Big Top

Smitten by love for the circus as a boy, I saved anything that would remind me of my pleasurable experiences. Nothing concerning the circus was too commonplace to discard—tickets, programs, handbills announcing its arrival, even ads clipped from local newspapers.

That was in the 1930s, when every spring my hometown of Columbus, Ohio, witnessed repeated invasions by shows—each one preceded by "advance men," who

Fred D. Pfening Jr., manufacturer of bakery equipment, once bought a small circus and ran it for a year with a friend. He has served as editor of "Bandwagon," the publication of the Circus Historical Society.

spread around their advertisements. I managed to wangle introductions to some advance men, who slipped me company letterheads, extra copies of billposters (for walls), heralds (handbills), window cards (small lithographs backed with cardboard) and "couriers"—pamphlets that were packed with such circus lore as the natural histories of wild animals in the menagerie and biographies of the performers.

My love affair with the circus has been shared by millions of Americans since the first show opened in the United States in a Philadelphia amphitheater in 1793. Like the English model on which it was based, the first American circus combined skilled equestrians with the derring-do of acrobats, all under a permanent roof. After the turn of the century, traveling shows were performing in the open for rural populations starved for entertainment; by 1826, tents were coming into use and the big top was born.

From the 1870s through the 1920s, the circus was a principal source of popular entertainment, boosted by such flamboyant promoters as P. T. Barnum, James A. Bailey and the Ringling Brothers, who competed ferociously with one another until the merger of their attrac-

The international pageantry of four circuses consolidated by P. T. Barnum and James A. Bailey is displayed in this 1881-1882 poster, which was printed shortly after the shows merged.

Heralds, like this rare 1853 depiction of an equestrian show, were passed out as fliers.

tions in 1919 into the grandest three-ring show of all. Meanwhile, smaller but no less grandiloquent entrepreneurs brought make-believe and daring feats to tank towns, whistle-stops and big-city arenas—M. L. Clark and Sons, the Campbell Brothers, Adam Forepaugh (often spelled 4-Paw in posters), the Sells Brothers and the Wild West shows that made household names of Buffalo Bill Cody and Annie Oakley.

All these shows spent large amounts on their various types of printed advertising. Today, most collections consist of these materials as well as photographs, company records and show materials, and, in some cases, costumes or props.

Little of this memorabilia would have survived to collect but for the diligence of a few early enthusiasts. One, Richard Conover of Xenia, Ohio, left behind a stunning mass of circus items still owned by his family.

Among the prizes of Conover's collection are route

A Chinese giant fills this 14-by-48-inch poster, made for shopwindows. Very tall—or short—people from exotic lands were a circus staple.

This 1881 poster was printed by Strobridge Lithographing Company of Cincinnati, as were most of all surviving circus posters printed in Amer- *ica. Among the marvels illustrated are the Seven Southerland Sisters, who displayed their 5-foot-long hair in sideshows during the 1880s.*

books from Civil War times and earlier—diaries of the yearly travels of a circus. One, the 1835 route book of a pioneer show called the Zoological Institute, is considered the greatest of all circus treasures; only a single copy, housed in the San Antonio, Texas, Public Library, is known to exist.

Another well-known collector, Burt Wilson, was a Chicago clothing salesman whose business travels took him along the routes of the circuses. He spent his lonely hours in strange towns gathering and arranging songsters (booklets sold by clowns, containing lyrics for songs they used in their acts), menus that were printed for special occasions, sheet music, Christmas cards and Ringling Brothers programs dating from the 1880s. It took me eight and a half years to close the deal to buy that fascinating collection.

Most of the other great private collections have been dispersed. I periodically run across couriers and heralds that seem to have been part of a collection amassed by a Billy Allee in St. Joseph, Missouri, in the 1870s. The names and dates on the material indicate the period,

and its physical condition coincides with what is known of the subsequent history of the Allee collection. Sometime around the turn of the century it was purchased by another circus fan, John Grace of Kokomo, Indiana, and while in Grace's hands much of the collection was mud-stained by a massive flood along Wildcat Creek in 1913. The stains do not detract from the value of these artifacts, but in a way add to it, since they serve as clues to its former ownership.

Some antique dealers specialize in circus material, and museums occasionally work through them to sell duplicate items. Flea markets and estate sales in cities such as Sarasota, Florida, and Columbus, Ohio, which were the sites of circuses' winter quarters, have been a good source of early collectibles, although they have been pretty well picked over by now.

Finds of old material are unlikely west of the Rockies—circuses rarely traveled to that part of the country before the turn of the century. To the east, print shops that have been in business a long time are worth checking, even in small towns. They frequently did some work for traveling troupes; the advance men often ordered a bit of printing from local operations in hopes of receiving publicity in return in newspapers that the printers published. And large firms that did color lithography are likely to have had circuses for customers, although such firms as the Courier Company, Donaldson Lithographing Company, Enquirer Job Printing Company and Strobridge Lithographing Company did most of the posters in the 19th and early 20th centuries. When Strobridge was sold in 1961, stacks of unused circus lithographs were donated to museums.

Circus collectibles are likely to turn up in more unexpected places as well. One of my oldest pieces is an 1800 newspaper advertisement for the Ricketts Circus that I uncovered in a collection of 18th and 19th Century newspapers I purchased from an editor in Texas. My niece once picked up for me a rare 1879 poster—an advertisement for the W. W. Cole New York and New Orleans Circus—at an antique store in North Carolina. The dealer, thinking the poster a piece of old paper, sold it to her for the price of the frame—five dollars.

The value of existing collectibles depends not only on age, of course, but on the numbers available. Ringling Brothers printed thousands of posters prior to 1907, for example, but a fire that year destroyed the printer's warehouse with all its stock of remnants from previous years. Today, most of the available posters that predate the fire come from a collection once held by Charles Ringling himself. If you can find one of them, that provenance further enhances its value.

There is more to circus collecting than just history, though. The majority of circus collectors cherish the things they carry away with them from their visits to contemporary circuses—things that remind them of the smell of the grease paint, the roar of the crowd and the breathtaking excitement that no other form of entertainment can duplicate.

For related material, see the article on Currier & Ives in a separate volume of The Encyclopedia of Collectibles.

In prose that tests the limits of the hyberbole, Diavolo printed this poster in 1904 for promotion of his loop-the-loop, a daredevil routine that brought him great popularity for a dozen years, most of that time spent as a principal attraction of Forepaugh's Circus.

The gymnast-aerialist Lillian Leitzel, 4 feet 9 inches of charm and nerve, was depicted at the height of her long career in this Stro-bridge lithograph. Her luck ran out on Friday, February 13, 1931, when she plunged from her trapeze to her death.

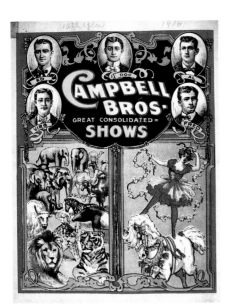

A menagerie and equestrienne grace the 1906 program of Campbell Brothers of Nebraska, one of the big circuses based in the Midwest.

Tickets were given to townspeople who helped the circus. Today, those from small shows, such as the middle three, are the more valuable.

A courier explaining the background of Pawnee Bill's Wild West show was printed in French for an 1890s European tour.

A harmless elephant is chained to suggest danger in this rare poster advertising a Southern circus in operation from the 1880s through the 1940s.

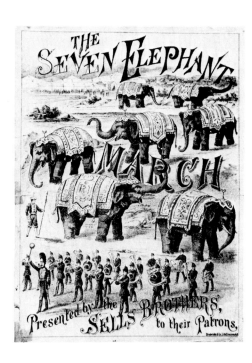

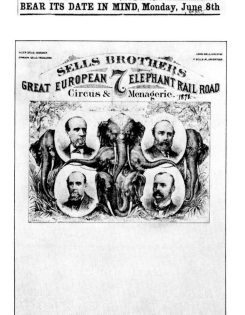

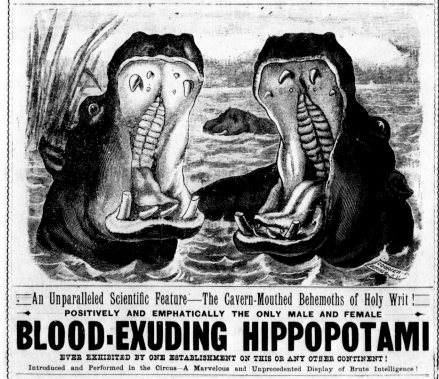

Examples of paper circus memorabilia include (clockwise from left) a Sells Brothers newspaper ad from 1885; a menu from a Fourth of July banquet for the Forepaugh-Sells troupe in 1907; sheet music from a Sells performance; a page from a rare advertising booklet showing two hippopotamuses with mouths agape, a pose that transforms the bulky but gentle herbivores into monsters; and a Sells letterhead, featuring the pride of the show, seven elephants, among portraits of the brothers.

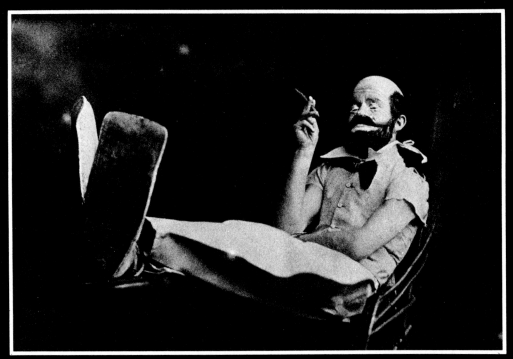

A clown's big feet demand additional rest, as is shown by Zolly Zora, a famous circus performer of the 1920s.

Clowns from the Sells-Floto Circus wear their identifying makeup for this informal group portrait in 1914.

Show Portraits

The circus and its denizens have always provided fertile ground for photographers—both amateurs and professionals. The best-known photographers of the circus were Mathew Brady, the great Civil War photographer; Harry Atwell, who took the picture at right, as well as thousands of photographs of the Ringling Brothers and Barnum & Bailey circuses; and Frederick Glasier, who traveled with circuses at the turn of the century.

Old photographic prints made directly from original negatives are very desirable. But the real prizes are the negatives—most are on old-fashioned glass plates now in museums. But the circus photographers were so prolific that an original plate occasionally may still be found.

A human pyramid, photographed in 1941, is established by Hungarian acrobats in their Middle European costumes.

A 13-foot billstand designed for advertising the Sells Brothers Circus dominates passersby in an 1894 photo.

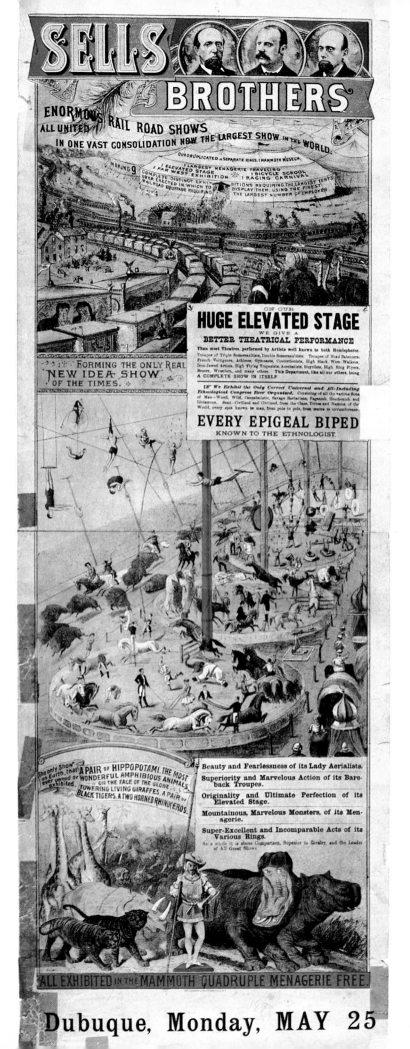

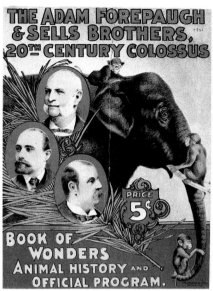

This program from Adam Forepaugh & Sells Brothers' "20th Century Colossus" dates from shortly after the troupes joined in 1896.

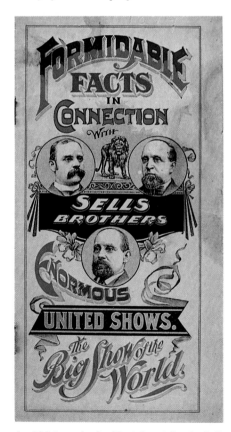

An 1894 courier booklet (above) for the Sells Brothers contains enticing and "formidable facts" on the menagerie and the show.

A Sells Brothers herald, or publicity flier (left), from the 1880s is prized because it was printed in four colors; most fliers were not in color.

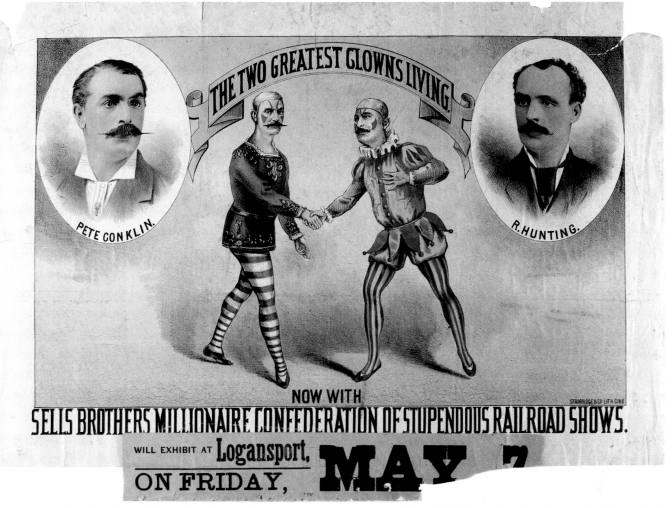

Famous clowns Pete Conklin and Robert Hunting clasp hands in the only known copy of this 1880s lithograph, with a "date tail" still pasted to it.

MUSEUMS
Barnum Museum
Bridgeport, Connecticut 06604

Barnum Museum
Medford, Massachusetts 02155

Circus and Local History Museum
Somers, New York 10589

Circus World Museum
Baraboo, Wisconsin 53913

Ringling Museum of the Circus
Sarasota, Florida 33578

COLLECTORS ORGANIZATIONS
Circus Fans Association of America
4 Centre Drive
Camp Hill, Pennsylvania 17011

Circus Historical Society, Inc.
800 Richey Road
Zanesville, Ohio 43701

Circus Model Builders and Owners Association
1056 Jefferson Avenue
Washington, Pennsylvania 15301

BOOKS
Chindahl, George L., *A History of the Circus in America.*
The Caxton Printers, Ltd., 1959.

Durant, John and Alice, *Pictorial History of the American Circus.* A. S. Barnes and Co., 1957.

Fox, Charles Philip, and Tom Parkinson, *The Circus in America.* Country Beautiful, 1973.

Rennert, Jack, *One Hundred Years of Circus Posters.*
Darien House, Inc., 1974.

Civil War Equipment
Mementoes of Gallantry and Courage

I became a Civil War buff at my grandfather's knee. The small New Hampshire town in which he lived mustered an entire company in the months after Fort Sumter, and Grandfather spent three years in that bloody conflict. As a boy I was enthralled by his reminiscences, and when only 14 I bought an 1863 Colt musket in a secondhand shop—at that time it was not considered an antique and it cost all of $1.50. I carried it home determined to get other relics like it and, as a secondary goal, to find out everything possible about their history. Both goals have colored my collecting since. I much prefer an average musket with a story behind it to a mint-

Dr. Francis A. Lord, retired Distinguished Lecturer in History and Curator of Historical Collections at the University of South Carolina, is the author of "Civil War Collector's Encyclopedia."

condition musket that was never fired. Seeking relics in remote areas, I have encountered bulls, a mad goat, vicious dogs, boars and poisonous snakes. More than once I wandered too close to a moonshine operation and considered myself lucky to leave in good health.

Civil War relics turn up all over the world. On a visit to England, I found a rare Alabama canteen and cartridge box in a town in West Sussex, carried there by an English collector. In Istanbul, at the Grand Bazaar, I was offered Colt pistols of Civil War vintage, testimony to the global trade in weapons of all kinds.

Although most collectors specialize more than I do in the types of memorabilia they seek, nearly all own at least a few weapons. While cannon tend to be inconvenient collectibles, it is comparatively easy to collect cannon balls. However, many contain explosives that, even after more than a century, are live and dangerous. Do not try to examine or deactivate them yourself; ask the police for advice. Muskets and revolvers may also be hazardous; handle all with caution and get expert assistance in unloading and deactivating them.

Some Civil War regiments marched to the stirring sounds of fifes and drums like these. The fife, made of rosewood with a silver mouthpiece, lies atop a handwritten fingering chart that was a New Hampshire infantryman's. The drum, also from a New Hampshire infantry regiment, witnessed the bloody battle of Chancellorsville, Virginia, in May 1863.

Firearms of this period are particularly interesting because the Civil War marked a transition in technology. Most of the earlier guns were smoothbore—like shotguns, their barrels were simply smooth tubes, lacking the spiral grooves, or rifling, that make the bullet spin and thus go in a straight path. All had to be reloaded by hand after every shot. The War saw the general introduction of weapons that fired many shots from a single load—including not only the six-shot Colt revolver and repeating rifles but also the first machine gun. And rifling, invented centuries before but little used, found widespread use as improved designs solved difficulties in loading powder and shot into a rifled barrel.

The principal gun of the North was the .58-caliber Springfield, first produced in the armory of that Massachusetts town. It was a rifled musket—a single-shot weapon very similar to earlier smoothbore muskets except that the barrel was rifled. The basic gun of the South was the British-made .577-caliber Enfield rifled musket, although the Union also purchased some Enfields. Other guns were imported from France, Austria, Prussia and Belgium. And many soldiers brought their own hunting guns. It is possible to find on the same Civil War battlefield the remains of a Revolutionary War flintlock, smoothbore musket alongside spent copper-cased bullets from a Spencer repeating magazine rifle.

Late in the War, the Confederate States issued locally made guns that today are considered great prizes. Some are stamped C.S. and also may bear the name of the maker and the place of manufacture; arms marked Tyler, Texas, and carbines stamped Morse, North Carolina, are particular rarities.

Since firearms are such popular Civil War collectibles, almost any old gun is likely to be passed off as a relic of that conflict. Especially suspect are Enfield muskets that look new or scarcely used; Enfields that had been ordered but not yet shipped from England when the War was over sometimes appear on the market as genuine battlefield relics. Also be wary of restored weapons; these are less valuable than pieces in their original condition. One inept collector destroyed the value of his Confederate guns by injudiciously reassembling them from a variety of parts.

From weapons, many collectors move on to accouter-

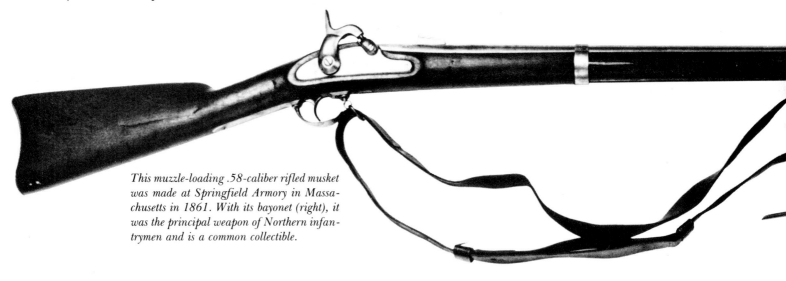

This muzzle-loading .58-caliber rifled musket was made at Springfield Armory in Massachusetts in 1861. With its bayonet (right), it was the principal weapon of Northern infantrymen and is a common collectible.

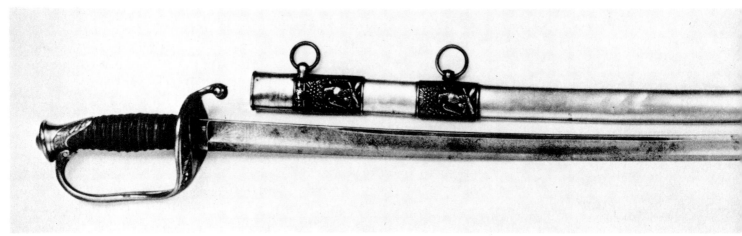

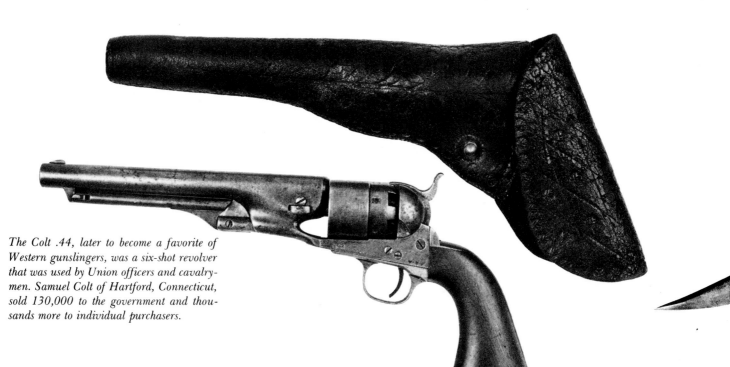

The Colt .44, later to become a favorite of Western gunslingers, was a six-shot revolver that was used by Union officers and cavalrymen. Samuel Colt of Hartford, Connecticut, sold 130,000 to the government and thousands more to individual purchasers.

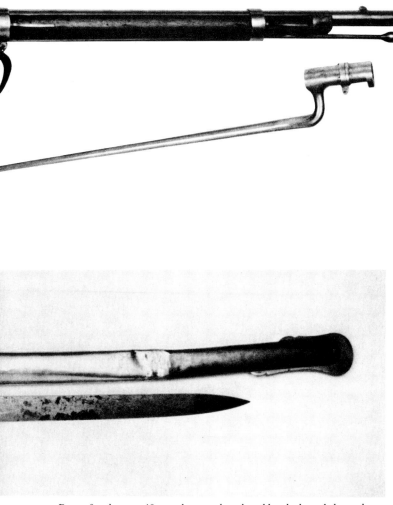

Part of a dress uniform, the sword and scabbard above belonged to a Connecticut artillery officer. Such "presentation" pieces were sometimes used in battle, but the shiny surfaces made wearers easy targets.

This nonregulation Confederate bayonet was patterned after the bowie knife, supposedly used by James Bowie, one of the heroes of the Battle of the Alamo in 1836.

ments—anything carried on a soldier's person, such as his canteen, mess gear and knapsack. One of the most curious items in my collection is a nonregulation wooden canteen used widely by Confederate troops *(page 78).* I bought it a number of years ago in a Southern antique shop for $1.50 from a proprietor who described it simply as a "wooden water bottle."

Uniforms—and the buttons, belt buckles and insignia that go with them—are a third major area of Civil War collectibles. Few authentic uniforms survive. Be especially wary of uniforms of Confederate gray made popular by Hollywood movies; many were made after the War for veterans organizations.

But of less perishable wearables—buttons, buckles and insignia—there are multitudes, and for the collector who delights in color and diversity of design, they can be an endless source of interest. They can also be extremely valuable: a single rare button, such as one from a uniform of one of the two Florida regiments, can be worth hundreds of dollars. Buttons cut from uniforms were traded among Civil War soldiers even before the hostilities ended, so loose buttons are likely to turn up almost anywhere, even in catchall boxes at flea markets. The problem is to recognize them for what they are. Military buttons with the names of the Waterbury Button Company and the Scovill Manufacturing Company, the biggest Northern suppliers, are likely to have come from the uniform of a Union soldier. But there are scores of makers' names on Civil War buttons, and the simplest way to identify them is to check them against the listings in Alphaeus Albert's *Record of American Uniform and Historical Buttons (page 87).*

There are so many reproductions of buttons and buckles—nearly all of them made for sale as inexpensive copies—that purchasers must be cautious. A few unscrupulous dealers manage to pass off replicas as the real thing, and an unwary buyer could pay $100 for a supposed Confederate belt buckle that in reality was worth five dollars. It is difficult even for the experienced collector to tell the difference if reproductions are made from the original dies and molds; the only distinction is that new ones look newer and are in better condition. But most copies come from new molds and dies, and designs may differ from the original in details that are recognizable after study of genuine articles.

One way of being reasonably certain that buttons or buckles are genuine is, of course, to dig them up from an actual battle site. They—as well as other metallic objects, such as mess gear, bullets and even guns—are readily located with one of the metal detectors sold for modest sums by many electronics stores. However, amateur archeology is subject to a number of limitations. It is illegal in the national and state parks that now encompass most of the major battlefields. And it should not be

These leather pouches, worn on the belt, held ammunition. The larger one carried cartridges—powder plus bullet—used in the .58 Springfield. The smaller pouch held caps to detonate the cartridge powder.

attempted on privately owned land—even assuming the owner gives permission—without guidance from a local historical society or the archeology department of a nearby university, since inexpert digging destroys the historic value of a site.

Much easier to find, since many of the items are likely to turn up at country auctions, is a simpler category of Civil War memorabilia: soldiers' personal effects. These include photographs and diaries, lockets and letters, and the little sewing kits called "housewives" that were sent from home by wives, mothers and sweethearts. Also included is the miscellany—tobacco, writing paper and pens, liquor and food delicacies—sold by sutlers (*page 85*), civilian merchants who accompanied the armies.

My own collection is especially rich in these personal effects. Many of them have been given to me by friends and relatives and have come with individual histories that add to their value. Many others are identifiable because the owner's name and regiment are inscribed on them. Union articles in particular are frequently stenciled with these vital facts. Using such clues, supplemented by regimental histories and family remembrances, I have over the years found out as much as I could about the original owners of the articles. Sometimes I have been fortunate. One of my prize finds is an 1861 manual of army regulations that was bought in a used-book store for $1.50 from a man who knew only that it was old. To him, the flyleaf signature of its original owner meant nothing, but any Civil War buff would recognize with a thrill the name Daniel Butterfield—a Union general who was a veteran of the Battle of Gettysburg, he composed a bugle call, "Extinguish Lights," that is now known everywhere as "Taps."

For related material, see the articles on Buttons, Guns, Knives and Model Soldiers in separate volumes of this encyclopedia.

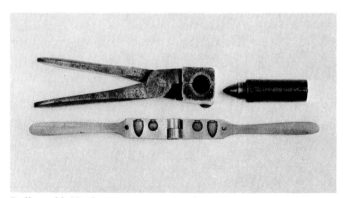

Bullet molds like these were unusual and were carried mainly by soldiers using nonregulation arms, for which ready-made shot was not supplied. The steel mold at top cast shot for a Union rifle; the brass mold below it cast .36-caliber bullets for a Confederate pistol.

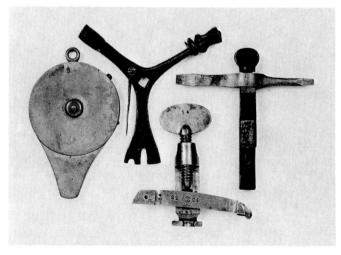

Typical of the tools needed to maintain and fire Civil War guns are, from left to right: a dispenser for percussion caps, a screwdriver-wrench for disassembling a Prussian musket, a small vise for repairing a rifle-firing mechanism and another screwdriver-wrench for an Enfield rifle.

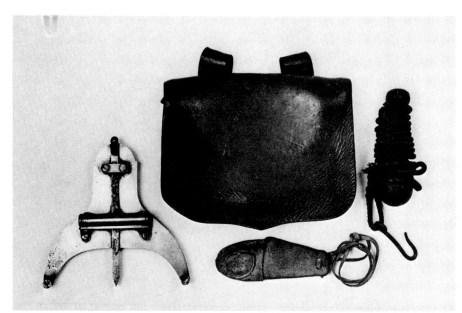

The kit of an artillery gunner contained, from left: a level to help sight the gun; a pouch for primers to ignite shell charges; a "thumb stall," which protected the gunner's thumb during a dangerous reloading step; and a lanyard that was pulled for firing.

This leather carrying case, about 12 inches high, was used to hold a single bag of powder charge for a 3-inch cannon.

Surviving specimens of ammunition are, from left to right: modern cartridges—percussion cap, powder and bullet all in one unit—for a carbine; a powder can to load a hunting rifle used by a soldier; a modern copper-cased cartridge for a Spencer repeating rifle; and an old-style, paper-wrapped cartridge, including only powder and bullet, for a .69-caliber regulation muzzle-loading musket.

Made of wood, the canteen at left is typical of the water bottles carried by most Confederate soldiers. The copper canteen is a better-quality import from Germany supplied to some Alabama troops, while the tin one covered with blue wool is the regulation canteen issued by the U.S. Army.

A tin mess plate displaying a camp scene was sent home by a Michigan soldier as a souvenir. The cup has a wire handle, probably improvised by the Confederate soldier in whose kit it was found.

The knife and fork at left are unmatched, like most eating tools men brought from home. The spoon came from Maine.

Amenities for Army Life

After watching young men march off to fight for the Confederate cause in 1861, a Georgia woman wrote that nearly all of them carried "a whole lot of spoons and forks, so as to live comfortably and elegantly in camp," and, she added, "their sweethearts gave them embroidered slippers and pin-cushions and needle-books, and all sorts of such little et ceteras." Most of the recruits from both North and South reported for duty with a jumble of such et ceteras. And the majority of them learned soon enough—usually after their first long training march—to reduce the number of these amenities to a less weighty minimum.

Beyond the comforts brought along or mailed from home, soldiers also had a friend in the sutler, a civilian merchant who supplied them with such items as strong drink, extra socks, sweetmeats and combs. The sutler had a permit—generally granted by a state governor as a political favor—to follow the troops from the governor's state. Most sutlers carried on their business from horse-drawn wagons, and sold their wares at whatever prices the traffic would bear. They were even equipped to make some items to order: the identification tags that many soldiers wore around their necks, forerunners of the dog tags of the modern army, were priority items just before a big battle. Without one a man knew that news of his death might never reach home. Sutlers also took their chances on survival. A sutler on the Union side could expect to be cleaned out by secessionist forces whenever a Rebel unit overran a Yankee camp, and vice versa.

Toilet articles were considered personal effects, to be supplied by the soldier. Clockwise from top are a shaving mug, soapbox, comb, razor, toothbrush, shaving brush and wood-framed mirror.

G. D. Smith's "housewife," probably furnished by one of the womenfolk he left behind, includes sewing notions for repairing uniforms and a brass name stencil for identifying new acquisitions.

The rattan-covered flask and the bottle once contained spirits. Along with smoking supplies, alcohol was one of the more important items that were supplied by the sutlers.

A discarded bayonet, its socket just the right size for a candle, was heated and coiled into a broad-based candlestick. The resourceful Virginian who made it probably used it in his tent.

These field glasses, together with their leather carrying case, were, according to a family legend, probably captured from a Yankee by the Confederate sergeant who owned them. Like nearly all good binoculars, they were European. The two brass pocket telescopes, probably expensive gifts from home, provided too little magnification to be of much use.

Apparently used as a wallet, this tooled calf-skin case with telescoping cover belonged to H. V. Polley of the 14th New Jersey Infantry. It was a gift from his family.

This folding camp chair of handsome turned wood has a sling seat of carpeting. It was among the personal camp furniture of a lieutenant in the 113th Pennsylvania Infantry.

The initials of the owner and his regimental designation are stenciled on the inside of the cover flap of this regulation U.S. Army knapsack. It was made of rubber-coated canvas.

The brass frame of this cap insignia placed its wearer in the 10th U.S. Army Corps; the red velvet center was the mark of the 1st Division.

This gold-plated cavalry insignia was worn by General Philip Sheridan's Riders, but this example may have been made after the War.

This cross-shaped cloth badge was worn by the 6th U.S. Army Corps. The "62" refers to the 62nd New York Infantry Regiment.

Union mottoes and patriotic emblems decorate two brass identification tags, which carry on the reverse sides their owners' names, home addresses and regiments. They were personalized by the sutler who sold them.

For a Confederate officer this buckle, wreathed in foliage, was comparatively fanciful. Union officers' buckles, more lavishly decorated, often featured such motifs as banners and American eagles.

This buckle was discovered buried in the undergrowth on the Chancellorsville, Virginia, battlefield. One hundred years earlier, its gleaming brass had offered a perfect target and it stopped a Confederate sharpshooter's bullet, which is still buried in its face.

This extremely rare six-pointed star, which was made of embossed brass and which looks like a sheriff's badge, was issued to a U.S. Army provost marshal, a term applied during the Civil War to all military policemen and not simply to their commander, as it is now.

This U.S. Navy cap belonged to an ordinary seaman and is extremely rare because the Northern Navy at the time of the Civil War was relatively small, numbering only about 50,000 men.

Confederate buttons identify the Navy (top row), Army General Service and Army Infantry (middle row), and the Cavalry and Louisiana Militia (bottom row). The Army General Service and anchor-embossed Navy buttons were made in England; the others, including the rare button reputedly designed for J. E. B. Stuart's cavalry, were Southern-made.

Epaulets replaced shoulder straps on formal occasions. These, in their tin storage case, belonged to a Union medical officer.

The regulation blue uniform jacket of an enlisted man in the Union Army was piped with color to signify his service. The yellow piping here shows that its owner was in the cavalry. Those in the artillery wore the same jacket trimmed in red, and infantrymen had light blue piping or none at all.

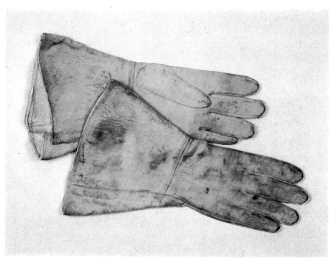

Soft buckskin gauntlets like these were issued to Union officers as part of their field uniforms. But a few months' active service generally wore them out, and only high-ranking officers could afford to replace them.

These square-toed leather boots belonged to Major S. K. Williams of the 2nd Ohio Cavalry. Their cutaway design protected the front of the knee while permitting the leg to bend in the saddle.

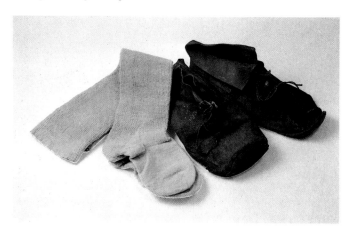

The woolen socks above belonged to a New York infantryman. The shoes, soles worn paper-thin, were a Confederate soldier's and were found where Stonewall Jackson campaigned around Frederick, Maryland.

A splendid silk sash, worn on dress occasions by an officer in a Connecticut infantry regiment, resembles those worn by officers on both sides — except for the embroidered identification, probably added by his wife.

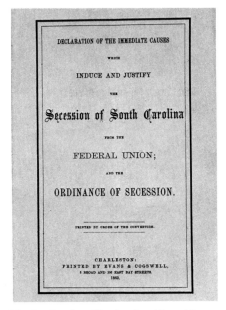

Spurs of brass like the ones shown above were worn during the War by officers and enlisted men who served in the cavalry and artillery, as well as by mounted officers in other services.

These brass pieces adorned the bridles of Union mounts. The heart-shaped ornament was fastened to a martingale, a device used to check the upward movement of the horse's head. The smaller, monogrammed rosettes were part of a bit.

The slightly irregular, utilitarian Confederate iron stirrup on the left was probably made by a hometown blacksmith. The factory-made brass stirrups were U.S. Army equipment for troops in the mounted artillery.

CLOTHING, &c.

	No.		No.
Knapsacks. . .		Drawers, prs. .	
Great Coat. . .		Bootees, prs. .	
Blanket. . . .		Boots, prs. . .	
Uniform Coat .		Stockings, prs.	
Undress Coat .		Money.	
Trowsers. . .			
Shirts.			

This check list was designed for making an inventory of the equipment and personal effects of a soldier admitted to a Union hospital.

Number of Bed:

Name: *Capt. A. J. Mason*

Company: *H.*

Regiment: *145th Pa Vols.*

Disease or Injury:

Date of Admission: *Dec 26th 1862.*

Date of Discharge. *Died Jan 12th 1863*

A Washington hospital document records the treatment of a Union officer fatally wounded in 1862 near Fredericksburg, Virginia.

DECLARATION OF THE IMMEDIATE CAUSES

WHICH

INDUCE AND JUSTIFY

THE

Secession of South Carolina

FROM THE

FEDERAL UNION;

AND THE

ORDINANCE OF SECESSION.

PRINTED BY ORDER OF THE CONVENTION.

CHARLESTON:
PRINTED BY EVANS & COGSWELL,
3 BROAD AND 103 EAST BAY STREETS.
1860.

The family of an Illinois colonel kept this copy of South Carolina's 1860 Ordinance of Secession, apparently sent home as a souvenir.

Pictures from the War

Though photography was hardly a generation old when the Civil War broke out in 1861, the new art form produced a remarkably full record of the conflict. Huge numbers of photographs survive in excellent condition and are easy to find.

Scores of enterprising photographers left the quiet of their studios to follow the armies. Driving darkrooms on wheels, setting up huge tripods and cameras even as shells whirred over their heads, they gave their own generation—and history—the first pictorial view of war.

Most of these men were Northerners; the rural South could draw on comparatively few commercial photographers. Certainly none were able to approach the massive operation of Mathew Brady, who neglected his fashionable portrait businesses in New York and Washington to invest more than $100,000 of his own money and years of his time in organizing the coverage of war.

Brady and his competitors produced prints by the thousands for sale to the public; some of them were double-image stereo views (below) that created a three-dimensional illusion in a stereopticon. But most of the Civil War photographs are portraits of soldiers, made by now-obsolete processes—daguerreotype, ambrotype, tintype—that produced only a negative on an opaque backing; it looks positive when held at an angle. Since many such pictures are more durable than prints, you may find them to be in better condition than the battlefield scenes.

Ambrotypes of a Union private and his wife, made before he left for the front, are in a case of gutta-percha, a kind of rubber.

Enclosed in a lidded gutta-percha locket, this tiny, inch-wide ambrotype portrait accompanied an Ohio soldier through the War.

THE WAR FOR THE UNION.

Maj. Gen. Burnside and Brady the artist, Head Quarters army of the Potomac, near Richmond, Va.

Photographer Mathew Brady, in a porkpie hat; General Ambrose Burnside, with a newspaper; and aides are seen in an 1862 stereo view.

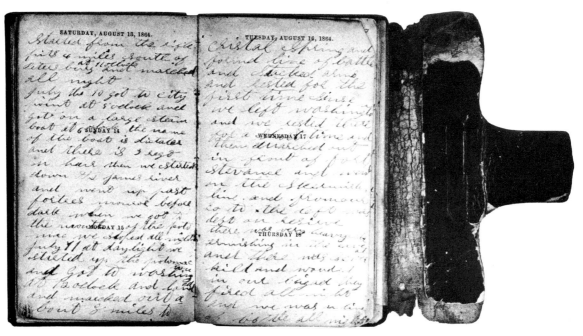

Soldier Edward Lewis Hoon of the 102nd Pennsylvania Infantry kept this diary from May 1864 until the following September, when he was wounded so badly that his leg was amputated. The diary records, among many events, his regiment's role in the battle of Winchester, Virginia.

These writing materials typify goods sold by sutlers. The mother-of-pearl-handled pen, the pencil and velvet case belonged to a Vermont infantryman killed in the 1864 Battle of the Wilderness. Two envelopes carry patriotic emblems, the third a view of Alexandria, Virginia. The writing box belonged to a soldier in the 45th Massachusetts Infantry. The ink bottle was found by a Rebel camp at Fredericksburg, Virginia.

MUSEUMS
Antietam National Battlefield Site—Visitor Center
Sharpsburg, Maryland 21782

Citadel Archives—Museum
Charleston, South Carolina 29409

Confederate Research Center and Gun Museum
Hillsboro, Texas 76645

Fort Sumter National Monument
Sullivan's Island, South Carolina 29482

Grand Army of the Republic Memorial Hall Museum
Madison, Wisconsin 53702

Historical Museum of the North and South
Acton, Massachusetts 01720

Manassas National Battlefield Park
Manassas, Virginia 22110

Museum of the Confederacy
Richmond, Virginia 23219

Smithsonian Institution
Washington, D.C. 20560

The United States Army Quartermaster
Corps Museum
Fort Lee, Virginia 23801

U.S. Army Ordnance Museum
Aberdeen Proving Ground, Maryland 21040

U.S. Army Transportation Museum
Fort Eustice, Virginia 23604

West Point Museum
West Point, New York 10996

COLLECTORS ORGANIZATIONS
American Society of Military Insignia Collectors
744 Warfield Avenue
Oakland, California 94610

Civil War Round Table of New York
289 Hyde Park Road
Garden City, New York 11530

Company of Military Historians
287 Thayer Street
Providence, Rhode Island 02906

Military Order of the Zouave Legion
of the United States
601 North M Street
Lake Worth, Florida 33460

PERIODICALS
Civil War Times Illustrated. Historical Times Inc.,
Gettysburg, Pennsylvania 17325

Civil War Round Table Digest. Civil War Round Table
Associates, Little Rock, Arkansas 72207

Military Collector and Historian. Company of Military
Historians, Warwick, Rhode Island 02886

North-South Trader. Publisher's Press, Inc., Langley
Park, Maryland 20783

BOOKS
Albaugh, William A., *Confederate Edged Weapons.*
Harper & Brothers, 1960.

Albaugh, William A., and E. N. Simmons, *Confederate Arms.* Bonanza Books, 1957.

Albert, Alphaeus H., *Record of American Uniform and Historical Buttons.* Published by the author, 353 Stockton Street, Hightstown, New Jersey 08520, 1969.

Boatner, Mark M., *The Civil War Dictionary.* David McKay Publishing Inc., 1969.

Bruce, Robert V., *Lincoln and the Tools of War.* The Bobbs-Merrill Co., Inc., 1956.

Catton, Bruce, *The American Heritage Picture History of the Civil War.* Doubleday & Co., Inc., 1960.

Edwards, William B., *Civil War Guns.* The Stackpole Company, 1962.

Gluckman, Arcadi:
United States Martial Pistols and Revolvers. Bonanza Books, 1939.
United States Muskets, Rifles and Carbines. Otto Ulbrich Co., 1948.

Hardin, Albert N., *The American Bayonet 1776-1964.* Riling and Lentz, 1964.

Kerksis, Sidney C., *Plates and Buckles of the American Military 1795-1874.* Gilgal Press, 1974.

Lord, Francis A.:
Civil War Collector's Encyclopedia. Castle Books, Inc., 1965.
Civil War Collector's Encyclopedia, Volume II. Lord Americana & Research, Inc., 1975.

Peterson, Harold L.:
American Knives. Charles Scribner's Sons, 1958.
The American Sword. Ray Riling Arms Books Co., 1955.

Ripley, Warren, *Artillery and Ammunition of the Civil War.* Promontory Press, 1970.

Clocks
Beauty in Time

It is hardly for practical reasons that people collect clocks. In one room of my house, for example, there are four antique grandfather clocks standing on the floor, nine shelf clocks on the mantel, two more clocks on the wall and smaller ones on tables. An inexpensive electric clock from the dime store is more accurate than the costliest clock I own, but I love the ticking of a dozen or more, each chattering in its own rhythm.

Most collectors fancy 18th and 19th Century clocks that chime or strike, their movements regulated by pendulums and powered by weights or springs. Many of these clocks are in wood cases of great beauty, like the shelf clock opposite. Some collectors, like myself, seek the bedside alarms and novelties of the 20th Century.

Some of the finest and most expensive clocks were handmade in Europe and are very desirable. But to many Americans, the most interesting collectibles are the mass-produced clocks of the 1800s—especially those made by a few now-famous Connecticut clockmakers.

The first American clocks were tall (7 to 9 feet) grandfather clocks—purists refer to them as "tall-case" clocks

---

Wesley G. Harding, a retired government attorney, began buying old clocks in the 1940s. His 60-clock collection is primarily American, although it also includes some foreign clocks.

—along with some shorter (3 to 5 feet) grandmother clocks. The cases were made tall to accommodate the weights, which hung from cords turning the movement, and the long pendulum that regulated timing.

The early tall-case clocks were hand-crafted by master clockmakers, who, with an apprentice or two, could produce perhaps 20 clocks a year, selling for $40 to $50 each in those days. Early grandfather clocks were made in a number of Eastern cities. Among the most famous makers were Peter Stretch of Philadelphia; William Claggett of Newport, Rhode Island; and Simon and Aaron Willard of Boston; most inscribed the firm name on the dial or movement, or glued labels to the

A clock of the type called pillar-and-scroll was made about 1818 by Seth Thomas and is a collector's gem, with its handsome, simple dial and hand-painted picture. The model shown here was produced in large quantities in the early part of the 19th Century.

A label from an early-19th Century clock proclaims that it was made in Plymouth, Connecticut, by Eli Terry. Terry, Seth Thomas' predecessor, invented the inexpensive clocks that revolutionized clockmaking.

cases. Today, any 18th Century tall clock, even in a case of painted wood rather than mahogany, is worth many times its original price. These clocks are considered fine antiques and are priced accordingly by dealers.

At the end of the 18th Century, with tall clocks so expensive, several clockmakers began to use wheels and gears made of wood rather than the more costly forged brass. Among them were Benjamin Cheney Jr. of East Hartford, Connecticut, and Gideon Roberts of Bristol, Connecticut. Later, a canny Connecticut lad named Eli Terry brought mass-production methods to clockmaking by standardizing parts and harnessing a stream to power his saws and lathes. In 1807, Terry received an order to make 4,000 clock movements for a manufacturer of clock cases. He finished in three years, much aided by his apprentice, Seth Thomas, who later became the most famous of the Connecticut clockmakers.

Even mass-produced tall clocks were too expensive for most people. So Terry turned his attention to improving the smaller clocks intended to stand on a shelf. He adapted gearing that permitted a relatively short pendulum and, to keep the mechanism working as long as a tall clock, he added gears and rigged the weight cords with pulleys so the full height of the case (a little over 2 feet) could be used for the drop of the weights.

Terry's shelf clock transformed the clock industry. Terry and Thomas mass-produced them with wooden parts; at $15, they were within reach of many Americans. These early shelf clocks (an example made by Thomas is shown on page 88) had handsome architectural cases with free-standing columns at the corners and a scrolled top. In 1839, Chauncey Jerome brought out a shelf clock with machine-tooled brass movements. His clocks were cheaper than the wooden-movement type and became more popular because brass gears wore less and were more reliable than wooden ones.

Part of the appeal of these 19th Century shelf and wall clocks comes from their imaginative cases: elaborate scenes were often painted below the clock face, as on the Chauncey Jerome clock on page 98. Some cases are commonplace rectangles, but many have fanciful shapes. One case resembles a church with a sharp Gothic arch at the top; another, the "beehive" has a rounded

The top portion of a tall, or grandfather, clock (below) made by British clockmaker William Troutbeck about 1710 has an engraved-brass dial and an elaborate floral design in wood inlay.

The white-painted dial indicates that this tall clock—unusual for its sweep second hand—was made around 1790. It was crafted by Isaac Brokaw of Bridge Town, New Jersey.

arch; "steeple" clocks *(page 92)* have sharply pointed wooden steeples at the corners, and so on.

In the 1830s, it became possible to make springs—long used for watches and some clocks—inexpensive enough for ordinary clocks. This eliminated the need for dropping weights and led to even smaller clocks, like the "blacks": mantelpiece clocks of pseudo-classic lines with pillars of marble, iron or enameled wood. They were followed by still smaller ones, such as the handsome desk and alarm clocks of the 20th Century.

To collectors, certain of these products of 19th Century Yankee ingenuity are particularly desirable. Banjo clocks top the list for many people. The earliest, handcrafted in the late 1700s by inventor Simon Willard or his brother Aaron, are as costly as tall clocks of that period, but later machine-made imitations—many marked with the intentionally confusing label "Willard's Patent"—are also valuable. Very desirable are mid-century versions made in several sizes by Edward Howard of Roxbury, Massachusetts. Almost as prized for their rarity are clocks with flat "wagon-springs" *(page 92)*, especially those made by Joseph Ives of Bristol, Connecticut.

Clocks from the most famous of the clock-factory founders, Eli Terry and Seth Thomas, are much sought after, especially the unusual pillar-and-scroll shelf type *(page 88)*. Somewhat less costly but very popular are schoolhouse clocks *(page 98)* produced by Seth Thomas and such other companies as New Haven, Ansonia, Welch and Gilbert *(page 100, box)*. This style was manufactured until 1940, and in 1972 was reintroduced by Seth Thomas as a collectors' item; the new clocks cost $180, roughly the going price for the antique version.

Much more widely available are kitchen clocks, particularly those that, unlike the example on page 99, were turned out in huge quantities. Although they may bring many times their turn-of-the-century prices, they can be bought for little more than the cost of a good modern clock, and they keep excellent time if carefully restored.

The most valuable in any of these categories of clocks are those clearly identified as the product of a famous maker—almost every company marked its name somewhere—and those consisting of original parts in working order. Some past repairs are likely to be visible, but value is reduced by recent and overzealous restoration—revealed in shiny brass or replacement parts that look too uniform to have been made in the 1800s.

Although old clocks in good condition—those with unmarred cases and accurately operating works—are costly, those that need restoring can be found at modest prices. Clocks that were inexpensive originally have wooden cases that amateur woodworkers can refurbish. Fixing the works requires a few tools, information on mechanisms that can be found in any of several books on clock repair—and the patience to tinker.

One collector has found several valuable examples by running ads in local newspapers offering to buy old clocks, no matter what the condition. Another bought at a back-road shop two 18th Century Pennsylvania tall-clock movements for $25 each and, for $90, a small clock made by Thomas Hall of London in 1760. Of course, all of the clocks needed repairs; the tall-clock movements lacked pendulums and weights and the Hall clock needed case rebuilding as well as drastic surgery on its movement. After the buyer had worked on them, those clocks kept excellent time—the Hall clock was accurate to one minute a week. A few years later he saw a similar clock for sale with a price tag of $1,700.

For related material, see the article on Watches in a separate volume of this encyclopedia.

This ornately topped grandfather clock, in the style of the 18th Century English furniture designer Thomas Sheraton, was made about 1815 by clockmaker Aaron Willard, brother of the more famous Simon.

A very early shelf clock, made about 1800 by David Wood of Newburyport, Massachusetts, has a mahogany case to accommodate pendulum and weights.

Two sharply pointed pillars flank the case of a steeple clock, a popular design that was devised by Connecticut clockmaker Elias Ingraham in the 1840s.

This gingerbread kitchen clock, made in Connecticut in 1875, bears the same sort of scrollwork trim popular on Victorian houses.

This 1850 clock was one of the last made with springs that, unlike the coil type used today, were flat "wagon" springs bent by winding.

A complex late-19th Century shelf clock made in Ithaca, New York, includes a perpetual calendar that even corrects for leap year.

This is a fine example of the rare acorn shape; the case is made of laminated wood. The painting on the clock shows lower Manhattan circa 1850.

A handsome example of the banjo wall clock, originally patented by Boston clockmaker Simon Willard in 1802, has fancy trim and a gilded eagle on top. This one was made by Willard's brother Aaron.

Lyre-shaped, this wall clock represents a variation on the banjo-clock design of Simon Willard. It was crafted in 1825 by John Sawin, who was Willard's apprentice.

This 1870 "regulator" clock, so-called because jewelers used the type to regulate other clocks, has a movement imported from Europe, principal source of precision handmade timekeepers.

A French clock rests in a porcelain case, 20 inches tall, enameled with landscapes. Ornate design distinguishes many French clocks of the 19th Century, when American cases were simpler wood.

The movement of an English "skeleton" is exposed to be seen and admired. These clocks, popular in Europe in the second half of the 19th Century, came with a glass dome to keep out dust.

A 400-day German regulator clock from about 1900 has a pendulum that twists instead of swinging. Its speed of oscillation is adjusted by tilting the mercury-filled tubes, which provide the weight of the "bob."

Traveler's carriage clocks, such as these three French models, had to be spring-driven because pendulum clocks run only if still and level. The clock at left, from about 1900, has an early digital dial. The other two, produced about 1860, have finely made striking movements.

A German cuckoo clock, made about 1895, is prized for its elaborate carving. It has a quail that announces the quarter hours while the cuckoo sounds hours.

Mass-produced clocks like the ones on these pages are easy to find and late models are reasonable in price. The rosewood case at right is unusual and desirable.

This clock, made about 1840 by Chauncey Jerome of Bristol, Connecticut, has a landscape painted inside the glass door. The S-curve-edge trim is called an ogee molding.

The drop octagon, or schoolhouse, design, a familiar fixture in classrooms for decades, is so popular that modern reproductions are common. This is an antique from about 1890.

A kitchen clock, made about 1900, includes a calendar, barometer and thermometer in an oak case embossed in fanciful Victorian Goth-ic. It sold new for under five dollars.

THE CONNECTICUT CLOCKMAKERS

Clockmaking was transformed from handcraft to mass production mainly in Connecticut. The most famous of the Yankee pioneers, including one from Massachusetts, are listed below by the name commonly associated with each—corporate names varied with business fortunes. Clocks made by any of these are desirable, although value depends on rarity and type.

Ansonia Clock Co.
Ansonia (1850-1929)

The William L. Gilbert Clock Co.
Winchester (1871-1964)

E. Howard & Company
Roxbury, Massachusetts (1840-1882)

The E. Ingraham Co.
Bristol (1857-1967)

Joseph Ives
Bristol (1810-1862)

Chauncey Jerome
Bristol (1824-1855)

The New Haven Clock Co.
New Haven (1853-1959)

The Sessions Clock Co.
Forestville (1903-1968)

Eli Terry
Plymouth (1807-1833)

The Seth Thomas Clock Co.
Plymouth Hollow
Thomaston (1853-present)

The Waterbury Clock Co.
Waterbury (1857-1944)

The E. N. Welch Manufacturing Co.
Forestville (1864-1903)

The unusual "Topsy" and "Sambo" clocks above, in enameled cast-iron cases, have eyes that blink as the clocks run. They were made by the American Clock Co. of Bristol, Connecticut, about 1870.

The "bobbing doll" clock patented in 1886 by the Ansonia Clock Co., one of the major Connecticut manufacturers, uses the ceramic doll in the swing as the time-regulating pendulum.

The humble alarm clock is today a specialty for collectors. Ansonia's "Bee" at left was one of the first ones made; in 1890 it sold for about $2.50. The Westclox Baby Ben at center dates from 1928 while the restyled one at right was made in 1953.*

MUSEUMS

American Clock and Watch Museum, Inc.
Bristol, Connecticut 06010

Greenfield Village and Henry Ford Museum
Dearborn, Michigan 48121

Museum of the National Association of Watch and
Clock Collectors, Inc.
Columbia, Pennsylvania 17512

Mystic Seaport, Inc.
Mystic, Connecticut 06355

National Museum of History and Technology
Smithsonian Institution
Washington, D.C. 20560

Old Clock Museum
Pharr, Texas 78577

Old Sturbridge Village
Sturbridge, Massachusetts 01566

COLLECTORS ORGANIZATIONS

The Antiquarian Horological Society
New House High Street
Ticehurst, Wadhurst
Sussex, England TN5 7AL

National Association of Watch
and Clock Collectors, Inc.
514 Poplar Street
Columbia, Pennsylvania 17512

BOOKS

Bailey, Chris, *Two Hundred Years of American Clocks & Watches.* Prentice-Hall, Inc., 1975.

Battison, Edwin A., and Patricia E. Kane, *The American Clock 1725-1865.* New York Graphic Society Limited, 1973.

Britten, F. J., *Britten's Old Clocks and Watches and Their Makers.* E. P. Dutton & Company, Inc., 1973.

De Carale, Donald, *Practical Clock Repairing.* N.A.G. Press, 1968.

Distin, William H., and Robert Bishop, *The American Clock.* E. P. Dutton & Company, Inc., 1976.

Drepperd, Carl W., *American Clocks and Clockmakers.* Charles T. Branford Company, 1958.

Dworetsky, Lester, and Robert Dickstein, *Horology Americana.* Horology Americana, Inc., 1972.

Maust, Don, *Early American Clocks: A Collection of Essays on Early American Clocks and Their Makers.* E. G. Warman Publishing Company, 1971.

Palmer, Brooks:
The Book of American Clocks. The Macmillan Company, 1950.
A Treasury of American Clocks. The Macmillan Company, 1974.

Tyler, E. J., *The Craft of the Clockmaker.* Crown Publishers, Inc., 1974.

Clothing
Treasured Hand-me-downs

When I was a child my parents took me to museums, like the Smithsonian, to see how people lived in earlier times. Ever since these visits, the clothes people once wore have had an irresistible appeal for me. Some people collect clothing for what it tells about social history; some approach collecting from the point of view of craftsmanship and the history of fabric and tailoring. Still others start with an interest in fashion and individual taste, becoming in time specialists in a single category: evening gowns of the 1920s and 1930s; "whites," or undergarments, of the Victorian era; men's wear; infants' dresses;

Mary D. Doering, who is curator of historical materials for the American Red Cross in Washington, D.C., began collecting costumes and accessories while she was still in high school.

---

creations from the workshops of such famous designers as Claire McCardell, Fortuny, Worth, Poiret, Vionnet, Schiaparelli and Adrian; or accessories—from aprons and lace collars to purses and shoes. Some become involved through an earlier interest in a related field like theater, photography or women's history. And some people are just lucky enough to inherit a trunkful of family heirlooms to get them started; essentially this is how I went from being an appreciative spectator to an active collector.

My first acquisition, given to me when I was 16, was a long dress that had been worn by a great-aunt around 1910; it was silk in a lovely shade of mauve, with black inserts bordering a lace yoke, and it had a captivating aura of long-lost elegance about it. My next treasure was a genuine paisley shawl that had been worn by my great-great-grandmother about 1850. I found it while rummaging in our attic. Not long afterward I chanced to pass a thrift shop that was showing in its window a beautiful black Edwardian blouse. For the modest price of about five dollars I made my first purchase. Now I had

This English "robe" is made of silk brocade woven in Spitalfields, an 18th Century silk-weaving center east of London. An embroidered sheer linen fichu, or scarf, fills the V neckline and ruffles appear below the elbow-length sleeves. A matching petticoat—remarkable for not having been lost—completes this collectors' prize.

three items spanning 60 years of fashion history and I was definitely and irreversibly hooked.

One of the first steps I took after that was to get a solid grounding in the history of costume. That meant reading books on the subject *(page 115)* and examining as many different costumes as possible by visiting museums and historical societies to train my eye. I joined the Costume Society of America, which operates under the auspices of New York's Metropolitan Museum of Art, to meet others interested in the history of clothing. I found that my preparation soon paid off both in the confidence gained in identifying and dating items and in establishing their relevance and value to my collection.

Most beginning collectors start, as I did, with late-19th and early-20th Century examples. You can always reach further back in time later if that is where your interests ultimately take you (I have since come to concentrate on 18th Century women's garments, though I also have representative examples of men's, women's and children's clothing from all three centuries). But meanwhile you will have tested the water in an area where prices are generally lower and the choices and sources of supply more numerous—clothing from these periods is available from a variety of sources, ranging from the specialty antique stores to the weekend flea markets.

However, some types of quite old clothing, such as men's waistcoats dating from the 19th Century, have survived in substantial quantities and are fairly easy to find. And an 1800 style of woman's dress, though rare, can sometimes be picked up inexpensively because dealers often fail to recognize it. This type is the charming high-waisted, low-necked Empire, or Regency, dress. These slender gowns, whose hemlines rose to ankle length after 1814, were frequently made of clinging, practically transparent white material like embroidered mull, a very fine muslin. Because of their simplicity the dresses are sometimes mistaken for nightgowns and are marked as low as one tenth their true value. It is always a good idea to pick through flea market lingerie boxes with this style in mind.

You will quickly discover that prices for period clothing vary enormously. At a Richmond, Virginia, second-hand store I once paid 50 cents for a lovely little ivory-colored-satin child's bodice made around 1840; it was

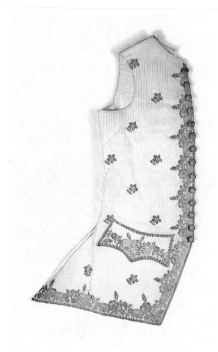 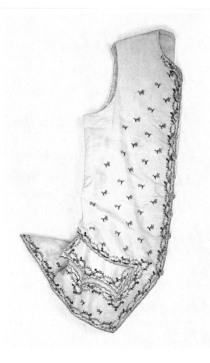

The elegant waistcoat at far left was made for a French gentleman around 1760; the brocaded silk is illuminated with edging and floral sprigs worked in gold threads. The silk for the waistcoat at left was hand-embroidered in China, then cut and tailored in England. The relatively small size of the floral motif was particularly fashionable in the decade after 1775.

lying buried at the bottom of a box marked, with true understatement, "CHEAP." But a very rare 18th Century dress may be priced at several thousand dollars.

The value of an individual item is usually determined by a combination of age, construction, condition, style, type of fabric and—in the case of garments sold by specialty dealers who know the market well—rarity. For most people who collect clothing, the preservation of the original sewing is important. A simple homemade dress made around 1840 with its original sewing intact is more collectible than a beautiful brocade dress dating from the 1700s that was completely remade for a fancy-dress ball around 1900.

General style usually indicates an approximate period. If you see a dress that clearly was made in America in the middle of the 19th Century, the nature of the stitches that hold it may pin down the date more closely, since machine-stitching did not come into general use until right after the Civil War.

Take a close look at the seams under a magnifying glass. In a row of stitches, do adjoining stitches come out of the same hole? If so, the seam is sewed by machine—unless the seam was backstitched by hand, in which case you will see that the stitches on the underside are overlapped. If they are machine-stitched but the individual stitches look quite crude and irregular in length, this is probably an indication that they were done on an early machine, before uniform stitch lengths were perfected in the mid-19th Century.

But it is easy to be fooled. A garment may have stitches so small and closely placed that at first glance they appear to be machine-sewed. The experienced collector will, however, recognize them for the fine handiwork of a first-class seamstress or tailor and reasonably date the garment before the mid-1800s. Do not make a judgment on one hand-sewed seam alone. Look over several parts of the garment—even after machine-sewing was well established it often was not used for sewing the finer, more visible parts of clothes, which were done by hand (just as they are today).

Look also for alteration to the original construction. Until well into the 19th Century, garments were altered—even by the rich—to accommodate changing figures or to catch up with a new style, since the investment in fabric in those days was far greater than the cost of remodeling. Very few alterations are completely successful, however, and as a result some of the beauty of the original design is lost.

Serious collectors might pass over a garment that through alteration has lost what they call its integrity; for the amateur there can still be great virtue in the item. I won my first 18th Century dress at an auction in London under just those circumstances. Heaped in a cardboard box was the English "robe" (from the French word for dress) on page 105—tagged with an estimated bid price equivalent to $50. The catalogue described the robe as having 19th Century alterations. That qualification usually means extensive cutting up of the bodice, a drastic reworking that discourages museum representatives from bidding. But when I inspected the robe carefully, I saw that the changes—which consisted of turned and basted-down bodice edges and the addition of two darts and several loops for lacing—could be undone without causing any permanent damage. On the day of

This silk dress and matching underskirt, dating to about 1770, is an example of a French sacque, or robe à la française, with back pleats that fall from the neckline to the hem. This style is one of the two principal ones that were fashionable during the 18th Century.

A brocaded silk dress with linen fichu, made about 1780, exemplifies the so-called English style. The dress has the characteristic fitted treatment of the back from the shoulder to the waist, an effect that was achieved through narrow, invisible tucks.

the auction I nervously bid my $50 and got a prize.

On still another occasion I came across the pair of elaborately embroidered 18th Century green silk stockings *(page 107)* in an auction catalogue that I received in the mail. The notation on the stockings lot indicated they had been altered, and the estimate of price expected was $35 to $50—similar stockings unaltered would have been worth hundreds of dollars. A friend in London successfully bid for me, and when the stockings arrived I found to my joy that they were much older—dating to perhaps 1680—and in much better condition than I had anticipated. The so-called alteration was not, I suspect, an alteration at all. The stockings were left open at the toes, with the opening nicely finished off; what the cataloguer had perhaps assumed was a neat repair job was probably the original design of the stockings—a 17th Century version of the one-size-fits-all method of manufacture.

Characteristics such as alteration techniques and construction details greatly affect the value of a garment from any period. But the period must be established first. And the ability to do that depends on a knowledge of the popular clothing styles described in the literature of the period and illustrated in contemporary fashion plates. This documentation most frequently described the clothing worn by the wealthy, who had the resources to acquire larger wardrobes. The garments worn by poorer people seldom survive, since they were usually worn out. The middle classes adopted the prevailing fashions to suit their own needs, substituting less expensive fabrics and trimmings.

During most of the 18th Century, for example, there were two common styles in women's dresses *(page 105):* a loose, fashionable French-style sacque, with pleats that hang freely from the neckline to the hem, and an English robe with a fitted back. The exquisite fabrics, most notably damasks and brocades, were displayed in wide skirts that were draped over hoops or side supports called panniers—literally baskets. The 19th Century was a period of great transition in styles of dress. Men's clothes evolved in the direction of sobriety while women's remained colorful and fanciful. The clothing of these periods has become difficult to find. Much more easily available—possibly even in family trunks—are garments of the 20th Century.

Before World War I, women's fashion interest moved to long and sweeping skirts gored to hold loosely to the figure. The tall and willowy, small-waisted full-bosomed look was much admired. Corsets were boned so as to throw the hips back and the bosom forward. Cascades of lace were everywhere. Skirts narrowed further after 1910, soon becoming the hobble skirt, which literally made walking difficult. There was even a kind of shackle, made of braid, that was sometimes worn below the

knees to keep the wearer from taking steps longer than three or four inches.

The 1920s marked the first act in a whole new style of dressing, and many interesting examples survive to document the dramatic changes that followed. Hemlines exposed the knee in 1925 for the first time in modern history. This fashion was denounced from pulpits across the country. In one short-lived evening fashion the skirt came down to the knees at the front and trailed on the ground behind. By the end of the decade skirts were down to mid-calf again.

Designer clothes from the 1920s and 1930s—and even later—are especially sought after by some collectors. Dresses from the salons of Dior, Chanel, Balenciaga, Norell and others can be discovered occasionally—sometimes in thrift shops, but more frequently in boutiques specializing in quality period clothes—and they are undoubtedly good investments. Owning such recent classics may tempt you to wear them but you do so at the peril of your collection. Textiles are extremely perishable, sensitive to light, humidity, dust and body heat and oils. The strain on an old garment can weaken or even tear the fabric.

Proper storage is another important consideration. Relatively lightweight clothing should be hung on padded hangers. A heavy garment, such as an elaborately beaded flapper dress, is best stored flat so that no strain will be placed on the shoulders or waistband. Be careful when storing clothing that the fabric does not touch the wood of a hanger or the walls of a trunk. Wood releases acids that can break down the fabric. Cardboard and tissue paper, unless they are specifically marked "acid-free," present the same danger. A bleach-free white sheet is a satisfactory liner for a wood or paper container. Be sure to wrap plenty of moth crystals in paper or muslin to discourage attacks from insects.

The process of cleaning antique clothing is also a tricky business and should be resisted unless it is absolutely necessary. But if you must, do not proceed without a careful analysis of the fiber content of the garment, the color fastness of the dyes, and the origin of the stain or discoloration. Any washing should be done by hand with a natural, pure soap.

As for repairing antique garments, most clothing collectors are reluctant to do little more than halt any evidence of deterioration as best they can. Extensive restoration can cause more problems than it solves. But if the garment is simply suffering from an open seam and it is possible for you to reproduce the original stitching with reasonable success, then the old adage follows: "a stitch in time saves nine."

For related material, see the article on Hats in a separate volume of this encyclopedia.

Easier to find than dresses are bodices like this one, made in France around 1780, of elaborate multicolored brocading on an unusual ground of stripes and flowers.

Rare English stockings of silk, with decorative clocks of silver embroidery, were made before 1700 to go with a silk dress.

Like many old shoes, this 18th Century English pair has silk uppers. They were shaped identically, and each could be worn on either foot.

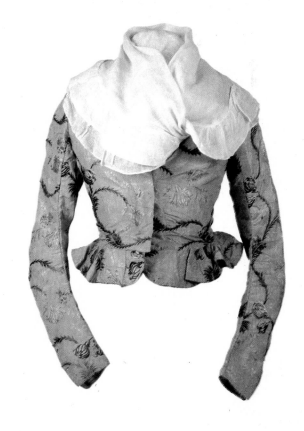

Long sleeves and fitted waistline date a French "Pierrot" jacket at about 1790, but the brocading on the silk shows it was loomed around 1745.

A child's linen waistcoat of 18th Century English origin is embroidered in "white work," a variety of delicate white-on-white stitchery.

An 18th Century English sheer linen apron is embroidered in white. Decorative aprons were an important accessory with day dresses.

How to Date Fabrics

Details of two Spitalfields silks show changes in technique and scale of design from a 1735 damask (left) to a 1750 brocade.

One of the ways knowledgeable collectors can make a fair estimate of the date of a garment is on the basis of the textile used. This is especially true of fine 18th Century clothing, whose fabric patterns tended to change more noticeably over the decades than did shaping, silhouette, bodice treatment and the like. The two very different-looking swatches of silk above are good examples.

The pattern above, at left, is typical of designs popular in European fashion between 1725 and 1750. The figures are noticeably large and formal. Flat woven in damask (named after the fabrics made for centuries by weavers of Damascus, Syria), the patterns were created by the contrasts between light and dark monochrome threads, the light figures by a lustrously smooth satin weave and the dark by the diagonal weave called twill; a similar play exists in reverse on the back.

After 1750 a new taste for delicacy was satisfied with brocades—patterns created by multicolor crosswise threads (the weft) at intervals on the fabric surface. The silk above, right, woven when brocades were becoming popular, bears a design that is more naturalistic, smaller in scale and gayer in effect than those on damasks. Unlike damask, brocade is not reversible.

With the invention of power looms in the late 18th Century and the ever-increasing variety of textile fibers available, clothing styles among the upper classes diversified. But some of the old patterns remained popular in 19th Century machine-loomed versions. To tell the later textiles from the hand-loomed ones requires close study, but the machines usually used finer threads and made a tighter, more even weave.

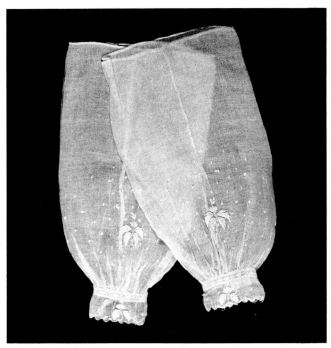

Cotton drawers like these—open like a split skirt except at the waist and ruffled cuffs—were worn from 1875 to 1900.

These embroidered undersleeves covered the forearm beneath the flared sleeves of English mid-19th Century dresses. They tied on at the elbow.

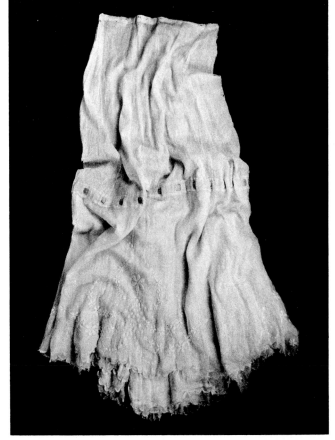

The needlework on this chemise, worn under a corset, shows it to have been made after 1850. Before then such garments were notably plain.

A turn-of-the-century American petticoat has a scalloped hem, hand embroidery and ribbon: elaborate trim typical of the Edwardian era.

The corded trim on the skirt of this faded-pink mohair and silk ball gown was fashionable for a short time in England around 1825, when waistlines were slightly raised above their natural level. The short sleeves, rounded neckline and fancy decoration indicate it was for evening wear.

The elongated V neckline and bodice, the long, narrow sleeves and the striped pattern of this somber silk day dress, worn in America around 1845, helped create the vertical lines typical of dress construction in that decade. Such a dress was worn over several layers of petticoats.

The full peplum and the flared sleeves of this velvet-trimmed satin "jacket bodice" were stylish in urban America in the 1850s.

A 19th Century embroidered satin waistcoat, made in England about 1840, retains decorative features that were fashionable a century before.

This classic paisley wool shawl was woven around 1850 in Paisley, Scotland, whence it got its name; the motif is actually of Indian origin.

A woman's riding jacket, made around 1880 in the U.S., is tailored in military fashion but with flared tails to accommodate a small bustle.

This conservative silk twill dress was worn for Sunday best in Wyoming in the 1870s, just after the voluminous crinoline had surrendered to the bustle. It consists of a separate bodice, skirt and overskirt and was machine-sewed except for the pleated trim.

This American day dress was fashionable in the early 1890s. The peculiar shape of the sleeves, widening toward puffed shoulders, provides the key to dating it. The printed muslin fabric, somewhat subdued for the Gay Nineties, was lightweight, suggesting that this was a summer dress.

An American turn-of-the-century day dress, originally worn by an admiral's wife in California, has a contrasting top and skirt. The bodice is black silk gauze with a border of jet beading; the skirt is brocaded silk. Its high neckline was in fashion for daytime wear from 1875 to 1910.

High-buttoned canvas boots (right) and leather ones with laced tops exemplify machine-made shoe styles popular in America around 1910.

A woman's wool coat with sprays of silk embroidery is loose and full, a shape stylish in America during the Edwardian era, around 1905.

An American mauve silk day dress displays the fullness over the bust found in styles worn around 1910. Typically, this style uses few stays but relies on corsets to give the wearer the popular S-curved silhouette. Black silk banding and lace complete the neckline and sleeves.

Gold kid shoes with a high, slightly flared heel and a strap across the instep were worn in the U.S. in the high-stepping Roaring Twenties.

MUSEUMS
The Brooklyn Museum
Brooklyn, New York 11238

Chicago Historical Society
Chicago, Illinois 60614

Los Angeles County Museum of Art
Los Angeles, California 90036

The Metropolitan Museum of Art
New York, New York 10028

National Museum of History and Technology
Smithsonian Institution
Washington, D.C. 20560

COLLECTORS ORGANIZATIONS
The Costume Society of America
c/o The Costume Institute
The Metropolitan Museum of Art
New York, New York 10028

BOOKS
Arnold, Janet, *A Handbook of Costume.* Macmillan, London, 1973.

Bradfield, Nancey, *Costume in Detail.* Plays, Inc., 1968.

Davenport, Millia, *Book of Costume.* Crown Publishers, Inc., 1972.

Kidwell, Claudia, and Margaret Christman, *Suiting Everyone.* Smithsonian Institution Press, 1974.

Kybalova, Ludmila, *et al., The Pictorial Encyclopedia of Costume.* Crown Publishers, Inc., 1968.

Waugh, Norah, *The Cut of Women's Clothes 1600-1930.* Theater Arts Books, 1968.

This embroidered silk coat was made in Peking to a European cut in 1928. Panels of older Chinese embroidery and rabbit fur trim it.

Coins
Metal Currency through the Ages

Well-designed coins are works of art that represent more than 25 centuries of man's history and for those reasons alone are worth collecting. The beautiful designs on ancient Greek coins speak eloquently of the artistic energies of that amazing people. A Roman coin proclaims the military might of a vast empire. A Renaissance coin announces the recovery of European art and commerce after the doldrums of the Middle Ages. Perhaps that bit of metal you hold in your hand is—who knows?—a coin once held by Plato or Cleopatra or Leonardo da Vinci.

Few collectibles combine so much history with so much beauty. And coins are a good investment. Even the moderately rare ones increase in value every year,

---

Richard Doty is the Associate Curator of Modern Coins and Paper Money for the American Numismatic Society. A three-time Fulbright scholar, he is the author of several books on coins.

---

and the coins of the United States and most other governments are always worth at least their face value.

Today's coins quickly become the collectibles of tomorrow. The loose change you had in your pocket little more than a decade ago contained coins that are already collectibles. If you have a small family hoard of old coins in the attic, it doubtless contains some coins that are worth more than their face value.

A couple of the basic lessons of coin collecting—which coins become valuable and why—can most likely be learned if you spill the change you have right now out on a table. It is likely to include, for example, two kinds of cents with Lincoln on the obverse, or heads, side. One is the "wheat" cent, so called because of the two ears of wheat on the reverse, or tails, side of the coin. The other shows the Lincoln Memorial on the reverse. The wheat

A scattering of coins from many eras and nations lies next to the collector's tools, a magnifying glass and protective envelopes. At bottom are a 1961 U.S. nickel and an Italian 500-lira coin of 1965. On the plastic envelope is a 1976 Malaysian ringget. Above it inside a case is a 12th Century bronze from India. Continuing clockwise are a 1512 coin from Cologne, a 1658 English crown and a Mexican coin of 1824. The flying-horse coin (center) is ancient Greek; diagonally above it are an 1857 U.S. half cent and a 1904 Panamanian 2½-centésimo piece.

cent, last minted in 1958, is vanishing from circulation. Eventually it will be found only at coin dealers', just as the Indian Head cent, common a generation or so ago, now survives only in the hands of collectors and dealers.

Coin collectors refer to a change in the design of a coin as a change of type. When a coin changes type, the older, supplanted design becomes increasingly scarce.

A change in the material from which coins are made can also render older coins more collectible, sometimes with dramatic swiftness. The chances are that your pocket change will not contain a dime, quarter or half dollar dated earlier than 1965. The reason is this: before 1965 these coins were made primarily of silver. But in the mid-1960s the price of the silver needed to mint the coins began to exceed their face value; that is, it took more than 25 cents' worth of silver to make a quarter.

The Coinage Act of 1965 required that thereafter coins be produced with less silver, and since then most have contained a copper-nickel alloy instead. Immediately, collectors (and hoarders hoping to make a profit on the silver) began pulling the coins out of circulation. Now anyone who finds a silver coin in his pocket is in luck, although he probably has not struck it rich. While silver 1950s dimes in uncirculated condition increased in value by more than 700 per cent in 25 years, that still made a 10-cent coin worth only 75 cents.

A paradoxical fact emerges from these examples: coins become more valuable and collectible when they no longer serve the utilitarian purpose for which they were made, that is, acting as a medium of exchange. Once out of circulation they become rarer.

Rarity is also influenced by another factor: how many of the coins were minted and released in the first place. For example, only about 1,000 cents with a flying-eagle design on the reverse were minted in 1856. One of those cents brought $2,000 when sold in 1978.

Age plays a part in a coin's rarity—with the passage of years coins get lost or mutilated. But age is not as important a consideration as you might assume. Some of the commoner coins of ancient Rome, although the newest are 1,500 years old, are still quite plentiful, for the good reason that Rome's Empire in its heyday embraced 100 million people, and staggering numbers of coins were needed to conduct trade—there was no paper money

THE ARGOT OF COINS

Coin collectors and the books they consult employ an arcane terminology. Some frequently used terms are:

BILLON: An alloy of copper and silver employed in ancient and medieval times.

BLANK OR PLANCHET: Piece of metal, generally round, that is struck with a design to make a coin.

BROCKAGE: A mis-struck coin with the same design on both sides, one normal, the other "incuse" *(see below)* and reversed.

CLIP: A coin struck off-center so that it is crescent-shaped, not round; this error generally adds value.

DIE: A piece of hard metal engraved with a coin's design, used to hammer the design onto the blank.

DOUBLE-STRIKE: A blurred coin accidentally struck twice during minting—rare and valuable.

FIELD: Background of a coin minus the design.

FINENESS: The proportion of precious metal in a coin—.900 silver means a coin 90-per-cent pure silver.

INCUSE: A design sunk into a coin rather than raised. The 1908 to 1929 U.S. gold quarter eagles and half eagles had incuse designs, as did some ancient coins.

KEY DATE COIN: The most valuable coin in a series, generally the one bearing the date when the smallest number of that type was minted. For example, the U.S. key date coin among U.S. Liberty Head dimes is the 1895 dime minted in New Orleans, since about 70,000 fewer dimes were minted there in that year than in any year elsewhere.

MINT MARK: A small mark, usually a letter or monogram, on a coin that indicates where it was minted. The most common U.S. mint marks are D (for the Denver mint) and S (San Francisco).

OBVERSE: The heads side of a coin, bearing the most important design, generally a portrait head.

OFF-CENTER STRIKE: A coin accidentally minted with part of the design missing.

OVERSTRIKE: A coin recalled by mint authorities and struck with a new design on top of the old; traces of the original design usually remain. Overstrikes were made, for example, when a new king took over and wanted quickly to issue his own coinage without acquiring new metals to mint coins in the usual manner.

PROOF: A coin minted for collectors. The mint takes extra care that the metal and dies be flawless.

REVERSE: The tails side of a coin, generally carrying the design less important than that of the obverse.

then. A coin commonly called an antoninianus, issued in vast numbers by the Emperor Gallienus (253-268 A.D.), has generally been available from coin dealers for about six dollars, far less than the flying-eagle cent of 1856.

The other principal factor that determines a coin's value is its condition. Understandably, a coin bright and fresh from the mint is worth more than a battered coin with date and design virtually obliterated by years of rubbing against other coins in innumerable pockets and purses. Uncirculated coins are valued for their pristine beauty and also because they are rare: most of the coins a mint produces do get circulated. A rare, uncirculated 1928 half dollar commemorating the Hawaiian sesquicentennial—originally selling for two dollars apiece in 1928—sold at auction for $1,000 in the 1970s. Few collectors want a coin that is in worse shape than what dealers define in their catalogues as good—the design worn smooth but not obliterated. Collectors naturally prefer coins classified as fine or extremely fine *(page 119)*.

Condition, age and the circumstances of issue all affect the basic criterion of a coin's desirability: its rarity. How does a collector find out how rare a coin has become? Fortunately for the beginner, coin collecting is a long-established hobby. There are dozens of reliable guides and books (a selection is listed on page 139) that spell out what to look for on a coin to determine its value. Some of these books are readily available at coin dealers' shops. There are guides and catalogues covering virtually every sort of coin you might wish to collect, from ancient Greek coins to modern U.S. issues.

Because the variety of coins is so great, almost all collectors specialize in particular types. The three most popular fields are discussed in the following pages. The first is ancient coins, which cover more than 2,000 years of the coin designer's art as practiced in the Mediterranean basin from the Seventh Century B.C., when the first coins were struck in Lydia, the western part of modern Turkey, to the fall of Byzantium in 1453 A.D.

A second popular specialty is foreign coins, defined as all coins that do not fall into the "ancient" category and were not made for circulation in the United States. Most American collectors of foreign coins specialize in British issues, Mexican and Canadian coins and those made in Europe, although some go in for coins struck in China throughout that nation's long history *(page 126)*.

The leading category for American collectors is, of course, U.S. coins. It is a rich field, too, despite the comparative brevity of American history and coinage.

Most beginning collectors pick one of these broad categories, and it is wise to avoid narrow specialization until you find what interests you most. Veteran collectors are often persuaded to concentrate on more limited areas, however, by the sheer volume of available coins. Some look for "numismatic errors"—such as the dozen

Grades: G to Unc

Crucial to any coin's value is its condition. Collectors recognize nine states; six common ones are shown at right by U.S. quarters. The best *(bottom, right)* is worth 60 times as much as the worst *(top, left)*. The states are listed, with abbreviations in parentheses.
GOOD (G): Main features and legend clear. May have nicks and scratches.
VERY GOOD (VG): High points of design worn. Features are clear, bold.
FINE (F): High points lightly worn. All details remain clear.
VERY FINE (VF): Modest wear only on high points. No scratches or dents.
EXTREMELY FINE (XF): Minimal wear even on high points.
UNCIRCULATED (UNC): New; has a hazy sheen.

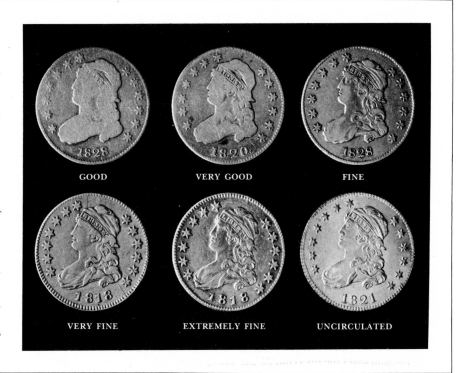

GOOD   VERY GOOD   FINE

VERY FINE   EXTREMELY FINE   UNCIRCULATED

or so 1943 cents struck in old bronze blanks instead of steel, worth perhaps $10,000 each. But the most common fields are coins categorized by type, date and time.

A type collector focuses on coin design. He might, for example, try to obtain an example of every different cent—Lincoln Head, Indian Head and so on—issued in the United States from 1793, when the first cent was minted, until the present. A date collector may specialize in one coin, say the long-obsolete American silver half dime. He would want a half dime from every year the coin was issued, 1794 to 1873. A thematic collector pursues coins from any country or period featuring a design theme. He might collect coins showing birds or animals; Greek coins abound in animal images, from lions to soft-shelled crabs. One collector, a hatmaker, looks for coins showing figures wearing hats.

To start a coin collection, all you need is a good magnifying glass to help see the small details of design, a book or two on the field of collecting chosen and a subscription to a coin magazine *(page 139)*. Coin dealers carry a wide range of display cases and boxes in which to keep a collection, but plastic or glassine coin envelopes suffice. They keep coins from scratching each other and also protect them from too-frequent handling.

To build the collection itself, you have to go beyond the resources of the change you get at the supermarket, although every collector carefully examines money that passes through his hands. Certain jobs—in banks and retail stores particularly—offer a special opportunity to look over large quantities of coins, and many people in these occupations build excellent collections for themselves by watching for rarities. However, most collectors buy their coins from dealers, shopping in person or by mail, or bid for them at auctions held several times a year by dealers in many major cities—among the most notable are Stack's in New York City, RARCOA in Chicago and Bowers and Ruddy Galleries in Los Angeles.

There is one special aspect of coins that sets them apart from almost all other collectibles: their great appeal to even the most ignorant thieves. While only a knowledgeable burglar will bother to make off with rare books or antique china, any intruding criminal will take coins. No expertise is needed to recognize their monetary value; no fence is needed to dispose of them. A dozen 1950 dimes are worth $1.20 in any store, although they might bring over $10 at an auction. Even coins that cannot be used in stores, such as an Athenian 479 B.C. tetradrachma, are valuable because they are made of silver or gold and can be sold profitably for their content of precious metal—one such Greek tetradrachma, melted down, yields silver worth about three dollars.

Such vulnerability to theft requires coin collectors to take extra care. If you acquire a worthwhile collection, do not advertise it; photograph it for identification, insure it, and when you are away for a period of time, store it in your bank safe-deposit box. After all, that is money you have there—and money which, despite inflation, keeps getting more valuable all the time.

Minting: A Process 3,000 Years Old

Coins are still made by essentially the same process that (aside from some old Roman and Chinese pieces that were produced by casting) has been used since the first ones were minted more than 2,500 years ago: a metal blank is squeezed between a pair of dies, one bearing the design for the obverse, the other the design for the reverse. The original dies are hand-engraved by master craftsmen today, just as they always have been, and the principal change in succeeding steps has been progressive mechanization.

In ancient times, the lower die was placed face up on an anvil—a bar of iron with a wedge-shaped lower end held steady by being driven into a large wooden block. The upper die was affixed to the bottom of another iron bar, which was positioned over a blank on the lower die and struck hard with a hammer. One blank at a time was thus squeezed between the top and bottom dies so as to press the

design into both sides of the metal piece at the same time.

Hand-hammering of coins gradually began to give way in the 1500s to the screw press. A massive screw was mounted vertically in a frame; the top die was affixed to the bottom of the screw, while the bottom die was set

The handsome but simple design on this 200 B.C. Greek drachma is typical of the detail struck with hand-hammered dies.

directly beneath in the frame. Men turned an iron bar, which tightened the screw, forcing it downward until it squeezed the design into the blank. The screw press assured a clearer and more uniform strike than that of a hammer blow and allowed engravers to produce elaborately detailed dies and coins, such as the Queen Elizabeth shilling *(below, left).*

The screw press continued to be used for two centuries until the introduction of mechanical power—first steam, then electrical—permitted a return to hammering in automatic punch presses. By 1797 steam presses were punching out coins like the English penny *(below, right).* In the 20th Century, coinmaking has been automated—the metal is cut into pieces, melted, cast into ingots, rolled into strips, slit into blanks, annealed, edge rolled, then struck by very large electrically operated hammers that are capable of minting eight million coins in an eight-hour shift.

Queen Elizabeth glares regally from an ornately decorated shilling coined between 1561 and 1566 by the then-new screw press, which gave clearer impressions of fine detail than hand-hammering.

The 1797 English penny above, with its clear if uninspired design, is the first national coin mass-produced by machines powered by steam. Machine-striking made possible a more exactly round coin.

Ancient Coins

Ancient coins, many of them superlatively beautiful, are readily available because of the staggering numbers made by the various Greek city-states, the Roman Empire and the Byzantine Empire. Hundreds of thousands have been found by archeologists in ancient ruins and even by farmers plowing fields. Most are in hoards—caches of coins hidden from thieves but never retrieved by their owners. As recently as 1963 a cache of 1,439 Fifth Century Roman solidi was unearthed by a farmer—in Hungary.

The most ancient coins, now prized museum pieces, date to the Seventh Century B.C., when the idea of coinage was invented simultaneously in China and in Lydia. Lydia (now in Turkey) was well endowed with gold and silver mines and is remembered chiefly for the legendary riches of Croesus, its last and most powerful king.

The prototype coins of the Lydians had a design on one side only. The man who had the first coins minted with designs on both back and front is said to have been a Sixth Century B.C. Athenian tyrant named Peisistratus, who spread his riches about Athens in the form of a silver coin with the profile of Athena, the city's patron-goddess, on the obverse and an owl, Athena's sacred bird, on the reverse.

All the Greek city-states followed this formula in their coins, depicting the patron-god or patron-goddess on the obverse, the city symbol on the reverse. Corinth, for example, also claimed Athena as patroness, but her profile is set off on Corinthian coins by a large war helmet. The reverse shows Corinth's symbol, the winged horse Pegasus. It is these symbols (along with, in some cases, a Greek-letter abbreviation of the city name) that enable collectors to tell the source of a Greek coin. Most of the city-states in Greece proper and their trading-partner cities around the Mediterranean minted silver drachmas, which are about the size of a United States dime, and tetradrachmas, slightly larger than a quarter. The designs are usually in handsome high relief, standing out more boldly than they do on modern coins, since the engravers incised their coin dies very deeply. Many of the designs are superb art; the heads of the gods are miniature rivals of the most glorious Greek sculptures.

Early Roman coins seem crude when compared with Greek ones, but their designs improved after the Third Century B.C. as the leaders of the Roman Republic enlisted the help of Greek engravers. A silver coin called a denarius, about half the size of a Greek tetradrachma, became the backbone of the Republic's currency.

The coins of the Roman Republic generally showed

A stylized head of a lion decorates one of the oldest of all coins, which was minted in the Sixth Century B.C. in Lydia.

Gold and silver coins from the ancient and wealthy kingdom of Persia display the figure of a king with bow and spear, symbolizing the royal power in war. Both were coined early in the Fifth Century B.C.

These beautiful coins illustrate the Greek practice of placing a deity on the obverse, a city symbol on the reverse. The head of Apollo stares from a coin minted in Rhodes about 400 B.C. The crab was the symbol of the Sicilian port of Acragas, where this coin was struck.

A magnificently modeled head of the god Herakles decorates the obverse of a large silver tetradrachma issued by Alexander the Great about 325 B.C.; it has a seated figure of Zeus on the reverse. Alexander, whose conquests reached as far as India, established some 20 mints in his empire, and his coins were widely used in the ancient world. Some experts believe the head of Herakles was inspired by Alexander's features.

This early Roman coin appears crude compared with the lovely coins minted by the Greeks. A heavy piece of cast bronze, issued between 240 and 220 B.C., it is about 3 ½ inches across and shows the double-faced god Janus, a patron of early Rome, who looks into the past and future.

animals or gods and goddesses, as had Greek coins. But with the coming of the Empire, most Roman coins were struck on the obverse with a profile of the current emperor, who came to be considered divine. Julius Caesar was the first to be so portrayed and each succeeding emperor memorialized himself in this way. The coins of the Empire—most common are large bronze pieces—name the emperor, whose profile is surrounded by letters around the circumference, but the coins are not dated. But since the emperor depicted was the one then in power, the names and profiles indicate the approximate date. You only need a list of the emperors with the dates of their reigns to know approximately when a coin was struck.

After the western half of the Roman Empire fell to invading hordes from Northern Europe in the Fifth Century A.D., the center of civilization—and of coinage—shifted eastward to Byzantium (its capital, Constantinople, is today's Istanbul). Most Byzantine coins are crude compared with Greek and Roman ones. The engraving did not portray the emper-

A dime-sized silver denarius, the most common of Rome's early struck coins, has a portrait of Roma, the protective goddess of the city.

or's face realistically, in dramatic, finely wrought relief as had Roman coins, but was flat, stylized and conventional. This eastern part of the Byzantine Empire became officially Christian in the Fourth Century, and Christian figures first appear on Byzantine coins, many with crude but moving images of Christ and the Virgin.

Two other ancient Middle Eastern civilizations also produced coins—the Parthians, who, in about 100 B.C., controlled the land between the Euphrates River and distant Afghanistan, and the Sassanians, who built an empire on the ruins of Parthia between 224 and 637 A.D. The Parthian coinage at first looked Greek, but later took on a nationalistic character, invariably showing Arsaces I, the first Parthian king, on the reverse. Sassanian coins have symbols of the sun-worshipping Zoroastrian faith, such as an eternal fire, on the reverse, and stylized portraits of elaborately costumed kings on the obverse. Gone, unfortunately, was the austere simplicity of the Greek ideal, when gods looked like men and men could aspire to be as the gods.

A gold coin struck in Egypt during the period 170 to 117 B.C. depicts what is believed to be the head of Arsinoë I, the wife of Egyptian monarch Ptolemy II. Plainly Greek in design, the coin was probably made by a Greek engraver, many of whom worked in Egypt and in Rome.

Roman Emperor Tiberius' mother Livia appears on this coin—probably a Biblical tribute penny, used to pay a tax levied on Jews.

Collectible Biblical coins include the large tetradrachma. Shown here are the obverse (above) and reverse of one minted around 98 B.C. in Tyre. Tetradrachmas may have been the coins that made up the 30 pieces of silver paid Judas to betray Christ.

Jewish copper coins such as this are mentioned in the Bible. They were the widow's mites that Christ used as examples of true giving.

A lean-visaged Octavian watches balefully from a denarius (left) minted around 40 B.C. during the civil uncertainty preceding his reign as emperor. All subsequent Roman emperors placed their portraits on coins of their reigns. In the aureus (center) Emperor Trajan (98-117 A.D.) receives the blessing of the god Jupiter. At right is a solidus of Romulus Augustus, last of the emperors, who reigned from 475 to 476 A.D.

The bust of Emperor Hadrian appears on five coins from his reign, 117 to 138 A.D., when Rome, at the height of its power, issued coins in several denominations. From the left they are a bronze sestertius, a gold aureus, a brass dupondius, a silver denarius and a small copper as.

Flat stylized images of emperors decorate Byzantine coins (above). The reverse sides have inscriptions indicating value and date. On the bottom coin, XII means the 12th year of Justinian's reign—538 to 539 A.D.— and the M is a Greek symbol meaning the coin is worth 40 nummi.

The Byzantine gold solidus at top bears a cross, while the two bronze coins picture Christ's head and give His name in Greek. The Byzantine Empire, the center of Mediterranean culture after Rome's fall in 476 A.D., became officially Christian in the Fourth Century A.D.

China's Distinctive Coins

Old Chinese coins make unusual collectibles for a number of reasons. The basic design— round with a square hole—did not change for more than 2,000 years, for no apparent reason other than tradition. Coins were cast rather than struck, were made of such inexpensive metals as copper, brass or bronze, and were used in strings, tied through the holes, of about 100—a carry-over from older strings of pierced shells. The coin holes are square to hold the cast metal on a lathe for rounding the edges. Many coins had to be minted—two billion a year in the 17th Century—and even quite old examples remain easy and inexpensive to collect.

The inscriptions around the holes in these Chinese coins indicate the reign during which they were minted and help establish age.

The thin silver coins of two little-known ancient peoples, the Parthians of Persia and their successors the Sassanians, bear portraits less realistic than those on Roman and Greek coins. The smaller examples are Parthian silver drachmas that depict Mithradates II, who reigned between 123 and 88 B.C. The larger Sassanian drachmas show King Khosru II and fire symbols of Zoroastrian sun worship.

Ancient coins, like the ones above, are available in quantity. In the top row are, from the left: a Roman follis, Fourth Century A.D.; a Greek silver hemidrachma, Fourth Century B.C.; a Roman copper as, Second Century A.D.; and a Roman denarius, First Century A.D. In the bottom row are: a Byzantine follis, Sixth Century A.D.; a Syrian small bronze, Third Century B.C.; and an Egyptian bronze, Third Century B.C.

Wampum and Cowries: Symbolic Money

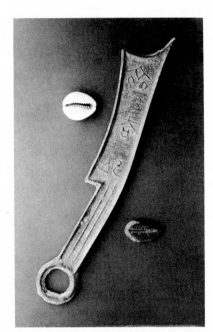

Cowrie shells and a toylike bronze knife were used as money in ancient China.

The oldest form of money is not coins but small portable tokens, generally of slight intrinsic value, that served as symbols for objects of barter. In many early societies, barter was based on cattle, and the animals served commerce as the primary unit of exchange. As a result, many words relating to money in modern languages are also related to cattle.

In English, "pecuniary" is derived from the Latin word *pecus,* the English "fee" from the Germanic *Vieh,* the "rupee" of India from the Sanskrit *rupa.* All three of these words mean cattle.

But barter is a clumsy way of doing business, especially when the main unit of exchange is as big as a cow. To facilitate trade, some cultures developed a pseudo-coinage of symbolic tokens that are considered a transition between the precious-metal coins of modern times and clumsy barter objects such as cows.

The best-known, perhaps, is wampum *(bottom, right),* the shell money of the American Indians. Usually made of polished and rounded bits of purple and white clamshell strung like beads, it had agreed-upon values known to the Indians, and soon learned by the early colonists, who used the native currency for trading both with the Indians and with one another.

Variants on wampum were used in many cultures around the world, most notably in ancient China, where cowrie shells were used as currency. By the Ninth Century B.C. China also had its own "utensil currency"—metal objects made to resemble implements such as knives and spades. Originally the implements themselves had been used for barter; it was but a short step to make a currency of symbolic utensils—knives that would not cut and spades too small for digging—that could be used for trade in place of the actual tools. The same idea had occurred to the ancient Aztecs; their utensil currency consisted of copper plates that were made to look like a hoe *(top, right).*

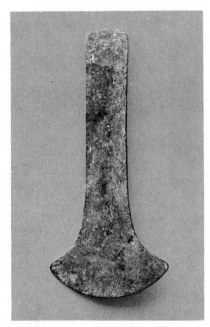

Shaped like a primitive hoe, this copper plate is an example of Aztec utensil money.

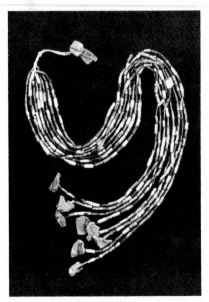

American Indians used colored wampum for adornment as well as for money.

Miniature spades like this one served as money in China from 403 to 221 B.C.

Foreign Coins

The field of foreign coins covers vast areas of territory—the world outside the United States—and great stretches of time, from the fall of Rome to the present. It embraces medieval coins, Renaissance coins and the coinages that were issued by scores of nations over the 400 years following the Renaissance. The field includes the coinages that were produced over hundreds of years by such long-lived countries as Britain and France—and the recent coins of the newly formed nations of Asia and Africa that have emerged since the Second World War. Also included are exotic coins from such far-reaching places as Indonesia or Malaya and—particularly favored by collectors in the United States—the coins of nearby countries such as Mexico and Canada.

There are a few recommendations that might help the beginner start exploring the labyrinth. It is probably best to rule out collecting the oldest coins in this group: the crudely made but historically fascinating coins of the early Middle Ages, the magnificent Gothic-style coins of the 14th and 15th centuries and the lovely florins and ducats of Renaissance Venice and Florence. All of them tend to be expensive to collect and are best appreciated in museums. The more readily available coins are those produced after about 1500, when commerce flowered all over Europe. Some collectors have specialized in the silver coins, about the size of a U.S. silver dollar, that were issued in the 16th and 17th centuries to facilitate international trade by many nations, especially Spain, which minted large numbers of them in the silver-rich Spanish possessions in the New World.

Other collectors have decided to specialize in British coins. It is possible to assemble coins illustrated with the portraits of virtually the complete line of British monarchs from the first Elizabeth to Elizabeth II without ruining the family budget. The coins of Britain's one-time colonial possessions also make a fascinating collection. The history of France can be traced in coins that date from the monarchy of Louis XIV through the Revolution, and from the Napoleonic era to the 20th Century and the two World Wars.

Still other collectors of foreign coins concentrate on neither recent nor distant history, but rather on the many beautiful issues being struck today by European countries or new nations such as Indonesia, Kenya or Zaire. Such coins are usually easy to acquire in their best, uncirculated state by ordering them directly from the mints that make them or from the mints' designated agents (page 130).

The crude designs on an early English coin called a sceat (left), minted sometime between 600 and 750 A.D., and a French gold triens of the Sixth Century testify to the decline of coinmaking in the Dark Ages.

The improvement in coin design toward the end of medieval times shines from the French coin (top), made about 1260, and the British sovereign, which shows Henry VII, king from 1485 to 1509, regally enthroned.

THE MINTS OF THE WORLD

To most governments, coin collectors are profitable customers. Many official mints sell at a premium the very desirable uncirculated specimens of new issues or proof sets—a half-dozen or so coins that are particularly carefully struck and wrapped. Many proof sets are made from special precious metals, and almost all are struck twice by highly polished and selected dies. In this superlative condition they are more valuable than other coins. And many are special issues made in small numbers to guarantee scarcity and boost value. If you wish to purchase coins from the national mints or their designated agents, write for information to the addresses below.

AFGHANISTAN
Royal Afghan Mint
Dehmanzan, Kabul

AUSTRALIA
Royal Australian Mint
Canberra, A.C.T. 2600

AUSTRIA
Österreichisches Hauptmünzamt
Postfach 225, A-1031 Vienna

BELGIUM
Monnaie Royale de Belgique
95 Rue de l'Hôtel des Monnaies
1060 Bruxelles

CANADA
Royal Canadian Mint
320 Sussex Drive, Ottawa 2, Ontario

CHILE
Casa de Moneda de Chile
Quinta Normal, Santiago

COLOMBIA
Casa de Moneda
Calle 11, No. 4-93, Bogotá

CZECHOSLOVAKIA
Czechoslovakia State Mint
Mennicy, Kremnica, CSSR

DENMARK
Den Kongelige Mont
Amager Boulevard 115
2300 South Copenhagen

EGYPT (U.A.R.)
Minting House, Abbassia, Cairo

FINLAND
Suomen Rahapaja
Katajanokanaituri 3, Helsinki 16

FRANCE
Administration des Monnaies et
    Médailles
11 Quai de Conti 75, Paris 6°

EAST GERMANY
Staatsmünzamt
Deutsche Demokratische Republik
Berlin, DDR

FEDERAL REPUBLIC OF GERMANY
Bayerisches Hauptmünzamt
Hofgraben 4, 8 München 1

GUATEMALA
Casa de Moneda
Avenida de Petapa No. 43-81
Zona 12
Guatemala City

HUNGARY
Állami Pénzverde
1450 Budapest, Pf. 6

INDIA
Indian Government Mint
Fort Bombay No. 1, Bombay

IRAN
Mint of Central Bank of Iran
Avenue Saltanatabad, Tehran

ISRAEL
Israel Mint
Myriam HaHashmonait St., Jerusalem

ITALY
La Zecca
Via Principe Umberto 4, Rome

JAPAN
Mint Bureau
1 Shinkawasaki-Machi, Kita-ku, Osaka

REPUBLIC OF KOREA
Korean Mint
407, Onchom-Dong, Dongrae-Ku
Pusan

MEXICO
Casa de Moneda
Avenida Casa de Moneda
Mexico City

NEPAL
His Majesty's Mint, Dharahara
Bhimsenstambha, Kathmandu

NETHERLANDS
's Rijks Munt
Leidseweg 90, Utrecht

NIGERIA
Nigerian Security Printing and
    Minting Co., Ltd.
Ahmadu Bello Road
Victoria Island, Lagos

PERU
Casa Nacional de Moneda
Junin 791, Lima

POLAND
Mennica Panstwowa
ul. Pereca 21, Warsaw

PORTUGAL
Casa da Moneda
Avenida Dr. Antonio Jose de
    Almeida
Lisbon 1

RUMANIA
State Mint, People's Republic of
    Rumania
Treasury Dept., Bucharest

SINGAPORE
Chartered Industries of
    Singapore, Ltd.
249 Jalan Boon Lay
Jurong, Singapore 22

REPUBLIC OF SOUTH AFRICA
South African Mint
P.O. Box 464
103 Visagie St., Pretoria

SPAIN
Fabrica Nacional de Moneda y Timbre
Jorge Juan 106, Madrid 9

SWEDEN
Mynvtrierket
Box 401, 631 06 Eskilstuna 1

SWITZERLAND
Swiss Federal Mint
28 Bernstrasse, Bern 3003

THAILAND
Royal Mint
Pradipat, Bangkok

TURKEY
T.C. Darphane ve Damga Matbassi
Istanbul

UNITED KINGDOM
Royal Mint, Tower Hill
London E.C. 3

A 1936 Italian 20-lira coin (above) and 1927 Albanian 100-franka-ari coin imitate classical Greek and Roman issues, as did some European coins in the '20s and '30s.

Two modern coins inspired by classic Greek designs are the 20-drachma Greek piece of 1930 (top) and a drachma of 1926. Both resemble the coins issued by ancient Corinth.

There is no reason a coin must be round; some collectors specialize in the distinctive shapes minted by many countries. These are, from the left: a Belgian Congo two-franc piece (1943), a Seychelles five-cent coin (1972), a Bangladesh five-poisha piece (1973) and a 50-new-pence coin (1970) from Britain. Odd shapes have a practical advantage: coins of similar size but different denomination can be recognized by feel.

The coinage of new nations or newly independent ones presents an opportunity for "before-and-after" collecting. The continuity of Jewish coinage is demonstrated in the specimens above. At left is a shekel minted in 67 to 68 A.D., during the first revolt against the Romans. Exactly 1,900 years later the state of Israel issued the lira at right with the same design.

The first coins minted in Australia, such as the two-pound gold piece of 1887 at top, are identical to British coins of the time; by 1910 the indigenous design at bottom was being used.

Coins of emerging nations, such as these Ghanaian and Zambian examples, often reflect nationalist pride. The 1958 penny at far left, issued soon after Ghana became independent, uses the new nation's name but retains the colonial British denomination, while the 1967 version specifies a Ghanaian denomination, one pesewa. Zambia, formerly Northern Rhodesia, added the native denomination ngwee to its old shilling.

The Traders' International Money

After the great explorers of the 15th and 16th centuries like Columbus and Magellan opened the way to trade between Europe and both Asia and the Americas, the need arose for currencies acceptable anywhere on the globe by people who knew nothing of the trustworthiness of the issuing country. This need was met by "trade money," coins of high silver content whose value was readily assessed.

Spain was a dominant mercantile power in the early days of world trade and its pieces of eight *(right)*, worth eight reales, were used as currency in the Americas and Europe. When the states of Latin America won freedom from Spain, they continued to mint coins of the same weight and value, such as the Bolivian piece *(below, left)*, which circulated around the world.

European nations besides Spain issued coins with the same silver content. The most famous is the Austrian thaler, first minted by Queen Maria Theresa in 1780. It became so popular in some ports that Austria issued it for 150 years, changing neither the design nor date lest suspicious merchants mistrust the authenticity of a coin that differed from the original.

When United States trade with the Orient increased in the 19th Century, the U.S. issued its own trade dollar, a coin fractionally heavier than the domestic silver dollar (by .0178 ounce) to match the silver content of the other internationally used silver coins. Even Japan had a dollar-value coin to facilitate trade with the Western ships that began to visit its ports.

These Spanish pieces of eight, the first internationally used money of modern times, date from 1652 (top) and 1681.

An 1848 Bolivian eight-sueldos piece, derived from the old Spanish piece of eight, bears so-called chop marks, symbols stamped on by Chinese merchants who tested and guaranteed its silver content.

The U.S. trade dollar at top is one of more than six million minted in 1875. At center is an 1876 Japanese trade dollar, at bottom an Austrian thaler minted in 1933 but, like the rest, dated 1780.

American Coins

The first American coins were minted in defiance of the law. When the colonies were young, the British Crown, like most governments then and now, insisted on retaining a monopoly over currency in all its dominions. As trade in the colonies increased, merchants found they could not get enough coins from the Royal Mint to do business with, so in 1652 they established a mint of their own in Boston.

The first coins were crude—thin wafers of silver with NE (for New England) on one side and on the other a Roman numeral denoting value. These were soon followed by little coins that were decorated on the obverse: first a willow tree, then an oak and finally a pine. These coins were minted over a period of 30 years, but all of them except the oak-tree twopence showed the date 1652. The date was a rather transparent subterfuge intended to lend an appearance of legality to the independent coinage, for 1652 was during the period of the English Civil War and Cromwell was in power. Since there was no British Crown to exercise its right of coinage, there presumably was no violation of the royal monopoly. The English monarchy, which was restored to power in 1660, was neither fooled nor amused by the stratagem, however, and forced the closing of the renegade mint. Tree coins—shillings, sixpence, threepence and twopence—are still available in good condition by collectors with hundreds of dollars to spend.

Since the colonies were blocked from minting coins of their own, they made up for the lack of proper British money by using foreign coins. The merchants of the Atlantic seaboard cities conducted trade with Dutch ducats, Spanish dollars, French écus and anything else that came to hand. All these coins were accepted because they had intrinsic value, that is, the gold or silver in them was worth approximately the coins' face value. So many foreign coins got into the American economic bloodstream that some were still commonly—and legally—in use more than 60 years after the colonists had won the Revolution, formed the United States and established a legal mint of their own. The most numerous of these foreign coins was the Spanish dollar, widely circulated throughout the New World. When the founding fathers came to consider a coinage, they decided that the basic unit would also be a dollar.

Several states stole a march from the federal government and minted their own coins, some of which are pictured below, before the Mint Act of 1792 established a national currency. The Act, passed just two years after the metric system of measures was established in Revo-

An odd spelling of Massachusetts borders the design that gave the pine-tree shilling its name. Among America's earliest coins, the 17th Century issue was minted in Boston from melted-down foreign silver, mostly Spanish.

The Vermont, New Jersey and Connecticut coins above date from the period in the 1780s when the Revolutionary War had been won, but the federal government had not yet established its own mint. The states therefore, for the only time in U.S. history, could mint their own coins. New Jersey coins were the first to bear the motto "e pluribus unum." Vermont copper cents (left), issued before Vermont was even a state, are very rare, but Connecticut issues are comparatively common.

lutionary France, called for a similarly rational decimal coinage—10 cents to the dime, 10 dimes to the dollar. Originally there were copper half cents and cents; silver half dimes, dimes, quarters, half dollars and dollars; and gold quarter eagles ($2.50), half eagles ($5) and eagles ($10). Half cents were discontinued after 1857; the silver half dime was discontinued in 1873 and the nickel five-cent piece (made of copper and nickel) was first minted in 1866; the last gold coin was struck in 1933. Otherwise, United States coinage today adheres to the pattern started in 1792.

Virtually all early U.S. coins followed the same general design: the head or figure of a woman standing for liberty on the obverse, and on the reverse the American eagle, or an olive wreath signifying peace. This pattern remained constant through the 19th Century and into the 20th; beginning in 1909 portraits of past Presidents replaced Lady Liberty.

This uniformity does not mean 19th Century U.S. coinage was static. Liberty was frequently redesigned. Some coins show her standing, some sitting, and some show only her head. The eagle became less fierce and then more so. Minor changes in lettering occurred almost yearly. Coins were issued off and on at more than a half-dozen mints named after the cities where they were located. All save Philadelphia regularly stamped their coins with an initial: D for Denver, S for San Francisco, O for New Orleans, C for Charlotte, North Carolina, CC for Carson City, Nevada. A short-lived mint in Dahlonega, Georgia, also used D between 1838 and 1861. There are also special issues such as coins commemorating significant historical events *(page 138),* and coins made by private companies during the 19th Century gold rushes, when so much gold was discovered that the government allowed some to be minted on the spot.

It is the complexity of United States coinage, with its periodic mutations and many mints, that makes the subject so fascinating. Unfortunately, collecting early U.S. coins can also be expensive. Some coins were issued in minuscule numbers. The mint in New Orleans issued only 720,000 dimes in 1894. By comparison, Denver minted more than 695 million dimes in 1976. So an 1894 dime mint-marked O for New Orleans may be worth hundreds of dollars if it is in good condition.

Many interesting United States coins, however, are reasonably priced. The large copper cent pieces, issued from 1793 to 1857, are inexpensive if minted after 1816, when mint runs increased. The Indian Head cents, issued for a half century beginning in 1859, are usually modestly priced and so are most issues of later Lincoln Heads. Examples of every type of cent—that is, every design ever minted—can be afforded if the rarer mintings are avoided. Most nickels are also within the reach of the beginner.

The Spanish "pillar dollar" (above), the most traded coin in 18th Century America, gets its name from the Pillars of Hercules in the reverse design. The example shown here was minted in Mexico in 1778. These fine silver coins were used legally in the U.S. until outlawed in 1857.

One of the first U.S. coins, the 1793 one-cent piece, shows Liberty on the obverse (top) and a wreath on the reverse. A Liberty head, although often redesigned, remained on all authorized cents until 1857.

The half-dozen 19th Century U.S. coins above all show the genius of James B. Longacre, the U.S. mint's chief engraver from 1844 to 1869 and perhaps America's greatest coin designer. They are, from top to bottom, the Indian Head cent, a two-cent piece of 1864, a small 1849 gold dollar, a silver three-cent piece, the first nickel (1866) and an 1858 three-dollar gold piece showing an Indian princess.

A Rocky Mountain decorates a $10 gold piece minted in 1860 by Clark, Gruber & Co., a mint that produced coins during the 19th Century gold strikes.

Designs by the celebrated American sculptor Augustus Saint-Gaudens cause these 1907 gold pieces to rank among the most beautiful coins ever produced in the U.S. The $10 eagle at left shows Liberty crowned with an Indian war bonnet. A more traditional figure of Liberty graces the $20 double eagle, at right.

These silver dollars present a capsule view of shifting tastes in coin design over the last century. Typical Victorian portraiture is represented in the silver dollar at left. A more modern Liberty adorns the new design at center, adopted in 1921. The 1971 coin at right commemorates the Apollo landing, showing an eagle landing on the moon.

COLUMBIAN EXPOSITION
1892-1893

PILGRIM TERCENTENARY
1920

INDEPENDENCE SESQUICENTENNIAL
1926

OREGON TRAIL MEMORIAL
1926-1939

VERMONT SESQUICENTENNIAL
1927

CONNECTICUT TERCENTENARY
1935

BRIDGEPORT CENTENNIAL
1936

BATTLE OF ANTIETAM
1937

BOOKER T. WASHINGTON MEMORIAL
1946-1951

The nine coins above are among the 48 types of U.S. commemorative half dollars issued between 1892 and the 1950s, when the minting of such special halves was discontinued. Some of the 48 were minted in more than one year—the Booker T. Washington coin (bottom, right) was produced from 1946 through 1951—and some were struck in more than one mint. As a result, a collector wanting a complete set with all mint marks and dates must acquire 142 coins. Commemoratives, a popular specialty among U.S. coin buffs, can sometimes be found at garage sales and the like since many people who were otherwise uninterested in coins saved them for their beauty and historical associations.

MUSEUMS

American Numismatic Society
New York, New York 10032

The Brooklyn Museum
Brooklyn, New York 11238

Buffalo Museum of Science
Buffalo, New York 14211

The Federal Reserve Bank
Philadelphia, Pennsylvania 19106

The Metropolitan Museum of Art
New York, New York 10028

Museum of the American Numismatic Association
Colorado Springs, Colorado 80901

National Bank of Detroit Money Museum
Detroit, Michigan 48207

The Newark Museum
Newark, New Jersey 07104

Smithsonian Institution
Museum of History and Technology
Washington, D.C. 20560

COLLECTORS ORGANIZATIONS

American Numismatic Association
P.O. Box 2366
Colorado Springs, Colorado 80901

American Numismatic Society
617 West 155th Street
New York, New York 10032

Canadian Numismatic Association
P.O. Box 226
Barrie, Ontario, Canada L4M 4T2

PERIODICALS

Canadian Numismatic Journal, Canadian Numismatic Association, Barrie, Ontario, Canada L4M 4T2

Coin Prices, Krause Publications, Inc., Iola, Wisconsin 54945

Coin World, Amos Press, Inc., Sydney, Ohio 45365

COINage, Behn-Miller Publishers, Inc., Encino, California 91316

Coins Magazine, Krause Publications, Inc., Iola, Wisconsin 54945

Hobbies, Lightner Publishing Co., Chicago, Illinois 60605

Numismatic Literature, American Numismatic Society, New York, New York 10032

Numismatic News, Krause Publications, Inc., Iola, Wisconsin 54945

The Numismatist, American Numismatic Association, Colorado Springs, Colorado 80901

World Coin News, Krause Publications, Inc., Iola, Wisconsin 54945

Young Numismatist, American Numismatic Association, Colorado Springs, Colorado 80901

BOOKS

Bowers, Q. David, *Collecting Rare Coins for Profit.* Harper & Row Publishers, Inc., 1975.

Carson, R. A. G., *Coins: Ancient, Medieval and Modern.* Hutchinson and Company Limited, 1962.

Chamberlain, C. C., *The World of Coins.* Hodder and Stoughton Limited, 1976.

Clain-Stefanelli, Elvira and Vladimir, *The Beauty and Lore of Coins, Currency and Medals.* Riverwood Publishers Limited, 1974.

Coffin, Joseph, *The Complete Book of Coin Collecting.* Coward, McCann and Geoghegan, Inc., 1973.

Doty, Richard G., *Coins of the World.* Bantam Books, Inc., 1976.

Forrer, Leonard S., *The Art of Collecting Coins.* Citadel Press, 1955.

Grierson, Phillip, *Numismatics.* Oxford University Press, 1975.

Krause, Chester L., and Clifford Mishler, *Standard Catalog of World Coins.* Krause Publications, Inc., 1977.

Porteous, John:
Coins in History. G. P. Putnam's Sons, 1969.
Coins: Pleasures and Treasures. G. P. Putnam's Sons, 1964.

Sutherland, C. H. V., *Art in Coinage.* Philosophical Library, Inc., 1956.

Wear, Ted G., *Ancient Coins.* Doubleday & Co., Inc., 1965.

Yeoman, R. S.:
A Guide Book of United States Coins. Western Publishing Company, Inc., 1977.
A Catalog of Modern World Coins. Western Publishing Company, Inc., 1974.

Zimmerman, Walter J., *The Coin Collector's Fact Book.* Arco Publishing Co., Inc., 1974.

Combs
Fancies for a Crown of Glory

Until the flappers adopted the boyish bob in the 1920s, women for centuries had worn their hair long and had fastened it with decorative combs. From the late 18th Century to the early 20th Century, such combs were the height of fashion, and many were beautifully made. Most were carved of tortoise shell or horn, although other materials also were used: bone, ivory, silver, cut steel and, toward the close of the 19th Century, Celluloid.

Designed to serve as jewelry, these combs are generally identified by the position in which they were worn—that is, as back or side combs. Expensive when new,

Alice C. Sawyer's collection of 400 combs reflects a professional interest as well as a personal one: for 10 years after her husband's death she owned and operated his comb company in Leominster, Massachusetts.

these combs were prized possessions, passed down as family heirlooms. Today they are sought after both as wearable artifacts and as mementos of a bygone era.

My interest in combs—especially American ones—grew out of my husband's comb company in Leominster, Massachusetts. Leominster has been known since the 1850s as a center of American combmaking. It is a hundred miles or so from West Newbury, Massachusetts, where American combmaking was begun in 1759 by Enoch Noyes, a young farmer.

The demand for Noyes's combs increased when the American Colonies embargoed British goods on the eve of the Revolutionary War, and in 1777 the War produced another bonus. One day a Hessian soldier, who had been captured by the Americans and was kept as a lightly guarded prisoner of war at a nearby farmhouse, came to Noyes. He was a combmaker and had brought his knapsack containing a kit of combmaking tools—saws, rasps, shavers and gravers. Noyes hired him.

Although the labor of sawing the teeth was progressively mechanized, decorative combs of tortoise shell and horn always required handwork. Both horn—the opaque yellow-gray horns of cattle or buffalo—and tortoise shell, from the hawksbill sea turtle, had to be softened by boiling. Some horn was "clarified," that is, made translucent by squeezing it in a press, so that it could be stained to imitate choice tortoise shell. All cutting, shaping and polishing had to be done manually. But in 1869 the first man-made plastic, Celluloid, was invented. Like horn, Celluloid could mimic tortoise shell. More important, its ornamentation could be machine-molded.

Today Celluloid has been replaced by newer plastics, but since nearly all modern combs are plain and utilitarian, they are unlikely to cause confusion to collectors. The real problem lies in differentiating between real tortoise shell and ivory and their Celluloid imitations. Genuine tortoise shell has random markings, and the color goes all the way through the material; tortoise-shell imitations generally have more regular patterns, and the pattern is often only skin deep. Genuine ivory has uneven striations; on imitation ivory the striations—produced by gluing together sheets of Celluloid—are straight and evenly spaced. In addition, the teeth of genuine tortoise-shell or ivory combs may be irregular because they are hand-shaped, while those of Celluloid combs betray a telltale machine-made uniformity.

Fine combs in good condition are scarce, and collectors must often use as much ingenuity in finding them as they do in identifying them. New England is the richest trove in America, especially right around Leominster, where many of the descendants of early combmakers still live. One of my favorite combs, a Celluloid back comb in the shape of an opened fan *(page 147)*, came from the attic of a Leominster librarian with whom I got into conversation one day; the comb had belonged to her mother. In antique shops I look through catchall boxes and poke into bureaus and display cabinets.

Although cracks and broken teeth diminish a comb's worth and can seldom be restored, a damaged comb may have value because of its style and workmanship. Remember that old combs should be handled with care; most become brittle with age. Temperature extremes can crack horn and tortoise shell, and heat or sun damages Celluloid. Cleaning should be done gently—I only use a damp cloth. But unless a comb is fragile, do not be afraid to use it; the beauty of a comb can only be enjoyed fully when seen against a crown of hair.

The 7½-inch-high tortoise-shell back comb at right, as intricately patterned as a piece of Alençon lace, was created by hand around 1825 for a wealthy woman whose initials are carved into the center of the design.

The 19th Century comb at right, 7 inches high, resembles tortoise shell but was actually made of horn clarified by or made translucent by pressing, and then stained.

Like many early American combs, this small 18th Century comb, 4 inches high, was carved in a plain style from raw, or unclarified, horn.

Dies were used to make the designs on this 5-inch, clarified-horn comb of the early 1800s, made of two parts joined by three screws.

Cameos in the classical Roman style are set in heavy gold mountings on this mid-19th Century horn comb, 4¾ inches high.

Black-dyed horn spheres are attached by screws to this 5-inch-wide comb of the same material; the design was in vogue during the Civil War.

This comb exemplifies the popularity of cut-steel jewelry in the second half of the 1800s. It may have been worn at an angle as a back comb.

This engraved silver comb is ornamented with a raised medallion that was encircled with rhinestones. The comb was made in two parts: first the teeth were cut separately from a sheet of silver and then they were soldered to the elaborately decorated top.

Shiny black beads of jet mounted on a metal frame were used to decorate the top of this 3 ½-inch-wide Victorian horn comb.

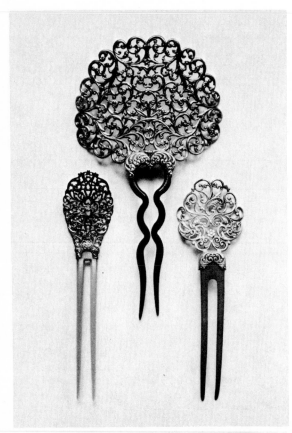

In this trio of hairpins from the early 1900s, all with silver filigree, two straight pins of horn flank a wavy Celluloid pin.

Elegant Hairpins

The hairpin—which in recent decades has become a utilitarian and virtually invisible hairdressing aid—has a long and even sparkling history. Renaissance women adorned their hair with two-pronged pins topped with gold, silver or jewels, and since that period, ornamental pins have been worn at various times whenever fashion called for hair piled high on the head.

From the late 18th through the 19th centuries, fancy hairpins were made of horn, tortoise shell or silver. Toward the end of this time, many of these pins were ornamented for evening wear with gold, rhinestones and even diamonds. Most of them were two-pronged hairpins, but there is also a long, single-pronged variety that sometimes pierced the fashionable chignons and topknots of the day. It is these elegantly decorated hairpins that are sought today, for they make handsome additions to a collection of combs, and they are generally less expensive to obtain.

An elaborately carved dragon set against a lacy openwork design distinguishes this hand-carved, 5¼-inch-high ivory comb brought from the Orient, perhaps by a New England clipper-ship captain.

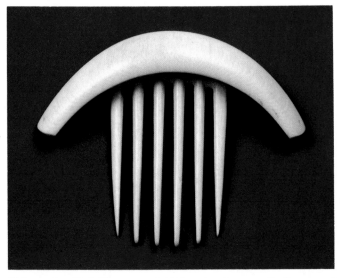

This curving 19th Century comb is hinged at the top to lie flat around the base of a knot. It is made of "vegetable ivory"—more even in color than real ivory—which comes from the nut of a South American palm.

This 5½-inch-high Celluloid comb in the Art Nouveau style of the early 1900s was die-cut; the colored rhinestones were hand-set.

The feather design on this 9½-inch, two-toned Celluloid comb reflects the early-20th Century fashion of wearing real bird plumage in the hair.

Close to 300 rhinestones, all set in place by hand, stud the fanlike top of this Celluloid comb made in the early part of the 20th Century.

Two layers of colored Celluloid, laid one atop the other, delineate the flowered design of this 9-inch comb from the early 1900s.

This fan-shaped comb, 8⅝ inches high and reminiscent of the Spanish mantilla combs, is mottled like real tortoise shell. The uniformity of the teeth and the openwork arabesques reveal that, in fact, it is an imitation; it was made of Celluloid in the early 20th Century.

Unlike real cameos, hand-carved of stone or shell, these are machine-molded as integral parts of this early-20th Century Celluloid comb.

The highly polished tortoise-shell comb with gold-plated ornamentation, above, could easily be mistaken for shiny plastic. It is 5 ⅛ inches high and was fashioned in Paris in the early 1900s.

This Celluloid comb in the shape of an open fan was designed to be worn with a small topknot and therefore has few teeth.

MUSEUMS
Greenfield Village and Henry Ford Museum
Dearborn, Michigan 48121

Mercer Museum of the Bucks County
Historical Society
Doylestown, Pennsylvania 18901

BOOKS
Flower, Margaret, *Victorian Jewellery*. A. S. Barnes and Company, Inc., 1967.

Walton, Perry, ed., *Comb Making in America*. Viscoloid Company, Inc., 1925.

Wilcox, R. Turner, *The Mode in Hats and Headdress*. Charles Scribner's Sons, 1945.

Comics
America's Favorite Fantasies

Comic-book collecting is serious business—or at least, semiserious. Collectors, dealers and comic-book publishers stage conventions each year to trade and sell. At one of the earliest of these "Comicons," in Houston, Texas, a California dealer, enraged because he had been offered only two cents each for the 3,000 *Marvel* comics that he had lugged from the West Coast, dumped all 3,000 of them into the hotel swimming pool. Barely a decade later the comics the dealer so cavalierly sent for a swim were worth an average of about three dollars each, or $9,000.

That dealer's loss demonstrates the abrupt rise in the cash value of old comic books. A complete set of *Marvel*

Richard E. Marschall, a former cartoonist and editor of comic books and newspaper-syndicate strips, is the author of "The Sunday Funnies."

Mystery comics—from No. 1, published in 1939, through the last issue, No. 92, published in 1949—was worth about $2,600 in like-new condition in 1971. Only six years later the same stack of 92 comic books, called a mint run, was worth more than $21,000, an increase of some 800 per cent.

The single comic book that has increased most dramatically in price is *Donald Duck Tells about Kites.* Published in 1954 as an advertising giveaway by Southern California Edison Company of Los Angeles, it was selling among collectors for about $20 in 1973. Four years later Donald's kite-flying lesson was commanding about $1,500, an increase of 7,500 per cent. An almost identical *Donald Duck* comic book was given away by a neighboring utility, Pacific Gas and Electric Company, and it is worth nearly as much.

Profit, however, is incidental to most collectors. The books of funnies replay childhood joys of reading about amusing characters and superhuman heroes. And the offbeat humor of *Powerhouse Pepper* or the supernatural fantasy of *Weird Tales of the Future* has special appeal to a number of collectors. In addition, comics often mirror trends in popular tastes, and occasionally even antici-

pate social developments. As a result, they have become a subject of scholarly study: university courses have been established to deal with them, and Ph.D. theses have been written about their influence.

As in the case of most collectibles, the desirability of a sought-after comic book depends partly on age. Comics are classified by time of publication into what many collectors call, rather ponderously, the Early Period, the Golden Age and the Silver Age.

The Early Period begins with the invention of the newspaper comic strip in 1895, when Richard Outcault created *Hogan's Alley* featuring the Yellow Kid, a homely waif in what appeared to be a yellow nightshirt. Outcault

Walt Kelly's political possum, Pogo, typifies the power of a comic character to generate a wealth of collectibles, including original art work, posters, buttons, records—and comic books.

Before there were periodical comic books there were comic strips like "Gasoline Alley" in newspapers. Original drawings for them are prized, as are color pages from Sunday editions; this example is from 1922.

An early adventure of Richard Outcault's bald-headed Yellow Kid—the first comic-strip hero—pokes fun at society dog shows. The rare tear sheet at left is from an 1896 issue of the New York "World."

Parodying Outcault's creation (top), Rudolph Dirks dressed one of his mischievous Katzenjammer Kids in the Yellow Kid's distinctive attire, a yellow nightshirt, in this 1898 strip for "The New York Journal."

These "Little Orphan Annie" Sunday pages are valued because of the variation in printing. Although color printing began in the 1890s, papers printed "Annie" in black and white, two color or full color.

Art work for a "Captain Easy" page in a 1934 Sunday newspaper is a rare survival. The Captain appeared in a comic book in 1939.

A prized "Little Orphan Annie" drawing of about 1945 has Daddy Warbucks, Sandy and Annie, with Asp and Punjab partly visible.

Art work using comic characters includes a "Teenie Weenie" newspaper panel, Kewpies on a postcard and Felix the Cat on a brochure.

In the first "Dagwood" strip—the 1930 art work is above—Bumstead introduces fiancée Blondie to his tycoon father. Dagwood then was a

slick-haired youth and Blondie a stereotypical dumb blonde, sharp contrasts to the personalities they developed over the decades following.

was immediately imitated, and over the following 40 years or so a multitude of now-familiar characters appeared to enliven newspaper pages—Moon Mullins, Mutt and Jeff, Popeye, Blondie, Mickey Mouse and Donald Duck from movie cartoons, and many others. These wonderfully funny comic strips were gathered into book form only very irregularly, if at all. There are *Moon Mullins* and *Mutt and Jeff* books with cardboard covers issued by virtually the only comic-book publishers of that period, Ball Publications and Cupples & Leon.

But such proto-comic books, along with rare examples of some of the artists' original drawings and some yellowed newspaper pages, are all that survive of the Early Period—and they constitute a special area of collecting. The oldest known original drawing of a *Mickey Mouse* strip for a Sunday color comics section, done by Floyd Gottfredson in 1937, was worth more than $2,000 a quarter century later.

The first of the modern paperbound comic books appeared as an advertising giveaway for Proctor and Gamble in 1933. Called *Funnies on Parade,* it, like the Cupples & Leon books, reprinted newspaper strips such as *Joe Palooka* and followed no regular publication schedule. The first series of comic books to be sold from newspaper racks in stores—for a dime each—followed in 1934. This was *Famous Funnies,* similar in content to *Funnies on Parade* but published regularly every month over a span of 20 years (including three No. 1s that were produced for different markets). About a quarter century after *Famous Funnies* discontinued publication, a mint run was valued at almost $5,000.

These and other early comic books contained funnies that were funny. But to collectors the Golden Age really began in 1938 with *Action Comics* No. 1, which not only introduced Superman, but also signaled a fundamental change in the nature of the comic book: from then on,

Toys from the Comics

In 1935, when the Hoge Manufacturing Company of New York City produced a lithographed windup Popeye in a boat with oars and rudder, the retail price was $2.50. As recently as the late 1960s its value secondhand was zero. But a decade afterward, a New York collector of comic-character toys turned down an offer of $3,000 for the one he owned.

No one except the children the playthings had been made for cared much about toys based on comic characters until comic books became prize collectibles, although these spin-offs date back to the very beginning of comic strips. The first character, the Yellow Kid, be-

came a doll in 1897 *(right)*, and nearly all successful inhabitants of the funnies since then have been turned into three-dimensional form. Most were made by large toy manufacturers in the United States, but many of them came from Japan and Germany.

The most desirable comic toys are the spring-wound mechanical ones like the Dogpatch Band below, particularly older ones of tin, a material replaced in the early 1950s by plastic. Also sought by some collectors are ceramic toothbrush holders decorated with Disney characters, and ceramic "nodders"— dolls equipped with pivoted heads that move when touched.

A Yellow Kid atop an Easter egg dates from 1897, shortly after the Kid was created. The doll is of plaster and was hand-painted.

Al Capp's Dogpatch Band puts on a musical act when this 1946 toy, now highly valued by collectors, is wound up. Pappy Yokum plays the drums, Mammy fiddles, Daisy Mae plays the piano, and a dressed-up Li'l Abner performs a tap dance.

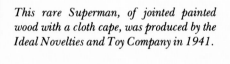

A tin Felix the Cat and his windup scooter were created in the early 1930s by the Nifty Co., one of several German firms that made toys based on characters in American comic strips.

This rare Superman, of jointed painted wood with a cloth cape, was produced by the Ideal Novelties and Toy Company in 1941.

A "Dagwood the Driver" tin car depicts the bumbling Bumstead learning to drive. Pictures of Blondie and Cookie are painted on the hood, and dog Daisy is in a cage in back.

This 14-inch Popeye doll, molded in 1935 from sawdust and glue, is hand-painted.

Comic books appeared in many formats from the 1920s to '50s. The 300-page Big Little Books, such as "Wash Tubbs" (upper left), used comic art to illustrate text. Other sizes predated the standardized form of "The Captain and the Kids," shown in a protective plastic bag.

many of the more popular ones featured heroes with supernatural powers. The most sought after of all individual comic books are those in which a new hero was introduced or, after introduction, was first published in a series with his own name: in addition to *Action Comics* No. 1, there are the 1939 *Superman* No. 1, in which Clark Kent and his alter ego first got a comic book all to themselves; *Detective Comics* No. 38 of 1940, in which Robin the Boy Wonder joined up with Batman; *Whiz Comics* No. 2 of 1940, which featured the introduction of Captain Marvel; *All-Star Comics* No. 8 of 1941, introducing Wonder Woman; and the 1941 *Captain America* No. 1, which introduced the patriotic hero of its title.

The superheroes did not end the popularity of humorous characters, many of whom first appeared in the early '40s. Again the most sought after are the issues in which a character is introduced: *Pep Comics* No. 22 of 1942 with Archie, the callowest teenager in all literature; the 1942 issue of *Animal Comics,* in which Pogo makes his entrance; and *Looney Tunes & Merrie Melodies* No. 1 of 1941, which brought Porky Pig, Bugs Bunny and Elmer Fudd to comic-book pages. There are, however, exceptions to the first-issue rule, such as *Donald Duck Finds Pirate Gold,* put out in 1942, six years after the first *Donald Duck,* but very desirable because it was drawn by Carl Barks and Jack Hannah, artists considered among the most gifted in the Disney studios.

After World War II another category of now-prized comic books supplanted the Golden Age. William M. Gaines—later to found the humor magazine *Mad*—dreamed up eight series, most of them horror tales: *Crypt of Terror* was followed by *Vault of Horror, The Haunt of Fear, Weird Science,* and so on. Some of the issues produced by Gaines and his imitators have become valu-

able, and later comics, from the period beginning about 1956 and called the Silver Age, are generally less desirable to collectors.

The comics of the Silver Age continued to star ghouls and superheroes, who now added intellectual pretensions to their physical powers. There were new turns toward satire, black humor and social consciousness.

Such desirable comics of the Silver Age as *The Avengers, The Incredible Hulk* and *The Amazing Spider-Man* are easier to find than those of the Golden Age, partly because they are more recent. But even the rarities of the Golden Age can be located by a sharp-eyed hunter. They date only from the late '30s and early '40s, and may turn up in garage sales, junk shops and attics. Most collectors find it useful to spread the news that they are looking for old comics. One man was rewarded when he followed up a telephone call from a friend of friends: amid an assortment of Golden Age wonders he found four copies of *Superman* No. 1, which he purchased for a total of $70. Each copy was actually worth at least 100 times its purchase price.

Such finds can be made almost anywhere in the United States and Canada—and surprisingly, in Europe. One of the largest caches of old comic books was discovered in 1976 in Copenhagen, where a warehouse had been packed with pristine comics apparently intended for distribution to U.S. Army bases. A party of Norwegian collectors carted off most of the treasures, including about 100 copies of *Uncle Scrooge* No. 1, one of the most admired of all the works of that Old Master of comic-book art, Carl Barks.

For related material, see the article on Toys in a separate volume of this encyclopedia.

Five collectors' treasures are these early appearances of heroes (and one heroine) in comic books of the Golden Age, from the late '30s to early '40s, when Captains America and Marvel, Wonder Woman, Superman and Batman battled criminals and Nazi evildoers. Particularly prized are issues introducing a character.

Among the most valuable of humorous comic books are those featuring animal heroes, particularly Walt Disney's creations and the satirical zoo of Walt Kelly. The first issues of "Mickey Mouse" and "Walt Disney's Comics and Stories" like the two at far left may be worth thousands of dollars. Kelly's Pogo and his alligator buddy, Albert, made their comic-book debut in the "Animal Comics," third from left. "Donald Duck" and "Uncle Scrooge" are prized partly because they were drawn by Carl Barks, whose work is favored by collectors.

Children's characters acquire adult personalities in such Silver Age comics as the "Fantastic Four," whose real-world problems complicate science-fiction derring-do. Howard the Duck finds humans perplexing, and Conan is a barbarian-philosopher.

Prized examples from the early 1950s, these issues of "Entertaining Comics" introduced gory violence and satirical humor of a type that shocked many people, leading publishers to adopt a censorship code.

The youth culture of the 1960s and 1970s found its expression in "underground comix," which mocked the Establishment and dealt openly with drugs and sex. Mr. Natural, the antihero of "Zap," was half guru, half con man. "Bijou Funnies" satirized conservative-liberal disputes, and "E. Z. Wolf" poked fun at urban intellectual pretensions.

MUSEUMS AND LIBRARIES
The Cartoon Museum
Orlando, Florida 32807

The Museum of Cartoon Art
Port Chester, New York 10573

San Francisco Academy of Comic Art
San Francisco, California 94116

PERIODICALS
The Buyer's Guide for Comic Fandom, Dynapubs Enterprises, East Moline, Illinois 61244

Classics Collectors Club Newsletter, 1930 West Warwick Lane, Roselle, Illinois 60172

Comics Journal, Fantagraphics, Riverside, Maryland 20840

BOOKS
Becker, Stephen, *Comic Art in America.* Simon and Schuster, 1959.

Blackbeard, Bill, and Martin Williams, eds., *The Smithsonian Collection of Newspaper Comics.* The Smithsonian Institution Press and Harry N. Abrams, Inc., 1978.

Horn, Maurice, ed., *The World Encyclopedia of Comics.* Chelsea House Publishers, 1976.

Lesser, Robert, *A Celebration of Comic Art and Memorabilia.* Hawthorn Books, Inc., 1975.

Overstreet, Robert M., *The Comic Book Price Guide, 1978-1979.* Crown Publishers, Inc., 1978.

Waugh, Coulton, *The Comics.* Luna Press, 1974.